Horus Templar

and the

Case of the Draft-Dodging Drone

E.L. WARD

Horus Templar and the Case of the Draft-Dodging Drone is a work of fiction. Names, characters, places, and incidents either are the product of the author's imagination or are used fictitiously. Any resemblance to actual persons, living or dead, events, or locales is entirely coincidental.

ISBN: 978-1-7370436-2-1

Table of Contents

Chapter 1 ______ page 5
Chapter 2 ______ page 9
Chapter 3 ______ page 19
Chapter 4 ______ page 30
Chapter 5 ______ page 40
Chapter 6 ______ page 49
Chapter 7 ______ page 62
Chapter 8 ______ page 72
Chapter 9 ______ page 84
Chapter 10 ______ page 92
Chapter 11 ______ page 114
Chapter 12 ______ page 128
Chapter 13 ______ page 135
Chapter 14 ______ page 146
Chapter 15 ______ page 152
Chapter 16 ______ page 163
Chapter 17 ______ page 168
Acknowledgements ______ page 180

"Weakness shows itself most in solitude."

- Magormissahr, *Referendums on the World, Vol. 57*

Chapter 1

DING-A-DING-DING

The bell over the door voiced its cheerful ding, heralding the twenty-nineth consult of the morning. "Allo, Sir!" Lucky called out, greeting the man as his silhouette passed before the bright office windows. Lucky noted the time on his pocket-watch, quick and discrete: 10:99:89. It was the third day in a row that his Dronehood Post received their twenty-nineth consult before 11 o'clock. He was sure that would look interesting on the scatterplot graph he'd been keeping...

"Good morning," the Human replied, sounding none-too-chipper. Humans had a curious way of coming off a bit on the down side, whenever they visited Dronehood offices. Lucky never really got that. Perhaps it was just that they were a proud race, and found no great joy in seeking help... even *good* help, happily offered. Or maybe he was just no good at reading their mannerisms. Maybe, deep down, they were actually every bit as glad to see him as he was to see them. Yes, that was almost certainly it...

"An' how may we be of service to you, this fine day?" Lucky asked.

The man sighed... something that would've seemed a sure sign of exasperation, if Lucky hadn't just ruled out the possibility. "Well, I don't know, but they stopped me up at the grocery market this morning." The man shook his head at some distant point in space. "It was such a simple thing. I wanted to buy five gourds, but they said I could only get four... unless I came here and filled out some sort of *form* or *permission slip* or something..."

"Ah, I see, Sir, I see!" Lucky said, flashing and bobbing his understanding, before he reached below the counter. "Seven in your family, I take it?" he called back up while he searched.

The man's face scrunched up. "No... just four. It's me, the wife, our boy of about ten and our baby daughter... who can't be bothered to eat almost anything besides mashed gourd."

"Ah, right you are, Sir, *four*!" Lucky chuckled nervously. "Beggin' your pardon for a clumsy limey; I convert the numbers so quick-like I sometimes forget which one to say aloud! But it's as I thought: You're after the ol' GenCom-0180871 Gourd-to-Citizen Ratio Exceeding One Permit!" He made a nudging sort of gesture in the air with one of his side-tentacles. "Eighth one in the last three months, you are."

"Well, isn't that something?" the man asked, rolling baggy eyes.

Even as he finished speaking, Lucky slapped a resplendently thick pre-stapled form on the countertop. Its papery goodness struck an interesting chord on the maple board – a melodious sort of sound somewhere between a *thwack* and a *thump*. "Ere you are, Sir... made to order! We've booths aplenty if y'd like to take a few minutes an' fill this out."

"*Minutes*?!" the man repeated back to him, flipping through the pages with an incredulous look. "A form like this will take me a week!"

Lucky laughed brightly. "I'm sure you're just putting me on, Sir, but you couldn't while a finer week away! It's one of our best forms; that I guarantee. Enjoy!"

"Yeah, right," the man replied over his shoulder, shaking his head and muttering as he headed back out. Lucky watched him go contentedly, seeing good had been done...

But he had only a few brief moments to share the Human's joy vicariously. For just as consult twenty-nine reached for the doorway, he was met there by another, shorter man on his way in. This new man, all in coat and hat, was a very dark shape against the light from outside, so that Lucky only dimly registered that the hat he was removing matched the outline of a police bobby. It caused Lucky a flutter of anxiety, such that he forgot to note the time of arrival. This, of course, only compounded his sudden discomfiture, knowing how the accuracy of his scatterplot had now been irrevocably devastated...

His scatterplot! Had it already seen its last entry?! It'd been weeks since Lucky unconsciously abandoned all such morbid fears. Now, at the mere sight of a cop, he couldn't help flashing with conspicuous doubt. He intently watched the thirtieth consult pause in the doorway, take a moment to wind his arm in an unfamiliar fashion, and finally, approach the counter...

"Is something the matter?" Lucky's distinguished superior, Clerk First Class Tangchuggle, asked him as he suddenly floated up, evidently taking quick note of his subordinate's unease...

"Looks like we've a policeman-caller," Lucky pointed out quietly.

"Nothing strange in that," Tangchuggle excused it. "Something like 0.011 percent of the city's population are policemen."

"Aye, but 'ow many come 'round on-duty, Sir?" Lucky asked forebodingly.

"Perhaps he's just here to advise us of some local trouble," his boss concluded. But his internal glow blinked as he considered Lucky. "Why should it bother you? You're not in some kind of trouble yourself, are you?"

"Never mind that," Lucky replied, fairly avoiding the question. "He's 'ere now; I best see what he wants." Lucky bobbed in a nodding sort of way as he moved out of sidebar to acknowledge the cop. "Top of the mornin', Guvnor!" he called, still sounding cheerful enough. "How may we 'elp you? We've every form, file and figure you could wish for."

"Nothing of the sort today, thank goodness," the policeman replied. He set his bobby on the counter, and held his shoulder while he rolled it and set his jaw. Lucky could see him now more clearly – he was an older man with an impressive silver mustache and a commanding voice to match. "I'm here on my own business, not yours. I'm looking for a drone by the name of..." he grudgingly reviewed a notecard in his shaky hand, "...Mobipetrolluck?"

Lucky progressed instantly from general misgivings to a kind of stunned terror. This was *really* it...

"That... that's *my* name, Sir."

"I see," the cop responded, wincing and grimacing while his shoulder went to work a third time, like he had it out of place and couldn't finesse it back. Of all the Human mannerisms Lucky couldn't hope to read, this had to be the most peculiar he'd yet seen. "I'm rather sorry to do this. But you're going to have to... going to have to come down to the station with me." With some effort, he wiped his brow, which was slick with fluid. "No doubt you're aware: There's a very serious matter to sort out, with regard to your citizenship, and your obligations abroad..."

"Don't tell him anything, Lucky," Tangchuggle advised sternly, before turning against the cop. "Now, see here, Officer: This man has put in nothing but good years of faithful service in this station since before I was transferred here myself... and that was some years even before the Twin Queens and their dratted war. Now the both of them have already recalled most of the Clerks they bore, and our ranks are badly depleted. The line has to be drawn somewhere! If it's left to only us foreign-born Clerks, there won't be enough of us to do the work. And I don't see that they have any right to conscript good Mobipetrolluck here... he who was born of Queen Yeminéya, the same as they."

"The *current* Queens would seem to believe otherwise," the policeman cautioned him. "I gather you're the one in charge here... and I can appreciate a few words put in for a faithful employee." He paused for another dramatic shoulder-roll. "But I must advise you not to interfere any further. Charges are being preferred against your fellow Clerk by *two* foreign powers." He turned to face Lucky himself. "You're in *deep*, Mr. Mobipetrolluck. You're liable to become a whole new front of the Queens' War in your own right. Accept it as some token of their intent, that the Deputy Constable himself was sent to apprehend you. The agents of North and South would accept nothing else, lest we let them take you into custody themselves. We couldn't have that." He grabbed his own arm while his face tried to wring itself out...

"Deputy Constable indeed!" Tangchuggle challenged. "Let's see some identification!"

Lucky tried to wave him down. "No, really Sir, it's alright! I *'ave* been dodging conscription orders – there's no use fightin' with 'im over it." He sighed, and began to float dejectedly out from behind the counter. "It's time I faced the music."

"Well said, Son," the Deputy Constable nodded. He turned to Tangchuggle, appearing pale and almost dazed. "But since you asked for it, here's my badge just the same, if it will mean a peaceful and speedy departure." Even as he moved to hold out his badge, he dropped it in a sudden convulsion. "Ek, clumsy. I'm... I'm afraid I'm not quite at my peak today." He wobbled and tottered as he tried to reach down for his ID. "Let me see if I can't..."

The officer didn't manage another word. He fell headlong in a heap on the ground. Lucky looked on with dread-curiosity as the man lay there, unresponsive, for several seconds...

"There's somethin' wrong with 'im, isn't there?" he asked his superior.

"Yes, I believe so," Tangchuggle replied gravely. "Something very wrong."

That was really all it took. Lucky – who'd spent most of a lifetime joyfully assisting those who stepped through the front door of the Office – now had a consult in more dire need than any he'd ever come across. There was no way for him to decipher what the Deputy Constable needed. But he could try to get him to someone who could...

"'*Elp*!" Lucky cried, desperately scooping up the stricken man in his tentacles and bearing him out of the Dronehood Post...

"'Elp!" his voice echoed in the streets. "This man needs 'elp!"

Chapter 2

"And here, after the metacarpals, we have the proximal phalanges," the instructor said, each toneless word oozing out of him glacially. Without benefit of a real diagram, he indicated each bone by pressing his pointer against the huge, menacing crimson flag draped at the front of the room, emblazoned with the skeletal sigil of the Cult: an image of a hand, with four bony fingers in black, set against the negative outline of a thumb...

Much as the nightmarish standard had initially made Art Mallard's skin crawl, watching the dull little man lazily poke at it now with his telescoping baton, all the while droning meaningless mumbo-jumbo at a snail's pace was steadily eroding any sensation beyond pure sleepiness. Propping his head up on one arm, the only thing keeping the private eye awake any longer was the chill of cold drool on his palm...

"Now, this is where things get reeeally interesting," the instructor claimed. Art's eyes rolled up under their heavy lids. Dimly did he register how everyone else in the room sat pressed into their desks, on the very edge of their seats. "See these bones after the proximal phalanges?" He let the question hang in the air for one or more eternities too long while he pointed to the next row of finger bones. "Those are the miiiddle phalanges." A look of astonishment began to draw the instructor's face back while the seasons went on changing. "Oh, but what have we heeere?" he asked, indicating the thumb. "There's no middle phalange at all on this one! We skip straight from the proximal to the distal!" He shook his head, the assembly breathing murmurs and shocked gasps. "Now I ask you good people: Could aaanything be more alarming than to confuse *this*..." he circled the thumb, "...with one of *these*?" His baton turned back to the fingers. Of course, everyone was horrified at the conceit of it all. The instructor only snorted. "But you must forgive a wild and wacky old professor – such as myself – for venturing a rhetorical question. The answer is, most assuredly: No. No... no... no. A *million* times... no." He nodded gleefully. "Thank you."

The room filled with thunderous applause from a universal standing ovation. Art – rudely awakened and more than a little confused – fumbled out of his desk and joined all the enthusiasm, lest his deep cover be blown. He checked around to see if anyone had noticed his delayed reaction, but all eyes in the dark room were fixed down to center stage. He gave a 'woo-hoo' and a fist-pump anyway, just to be careful...

"And thank *you*, Professor Buelschestein!" Supreme Elevated Grand Master Overseer Therodrux Mengaloid announced boisterously, still clapping as he invaded the stage from the left flank. He slapped a hand on the professor's shoulder, effectively affirming him as well as hijacking the program in a single action...

"Now, I think, you all begin to see the true extent of the dissimulation we've been living under," Therodrux went on, angling his speech up at the assembly as it slowly returned to reverent silence. "Your entire lives, you've been falsely taught, cleverly deceived, and brutally coerced into believing the thumb is a *finger*. How fortunate that we, the Digit Cultists, know better." His eyes passed over all of them, glimmering with a kind of invincible pride. "It has been my great honor to witness this knowledge pass on to each of you." He tightly curled a resolute fist. "Knowledge that will surely avail you against the rampant lies of the Inquisition, and all the rulers who willingly capitulate to them. I urge you: Proliferate these teachings. Spread them wisely... *cautiously*. But *spread* them. The truth will never have its day if we do nothing."

Then, standing very straight, Master Overseer Therodrux outstretched his arm, made the 'thumbs-down' gesture. All gathered did likewise. And as one, they began their pledge...

"I do solemnly reject falsehood, and the diverse powers of the world that seek to uphold it. I will speak no lie but what is necessary to protect the truth. I will suffer the deceit of our enemies only until I am strong enough to destroy it – and them – forever."

Besides the sigil itself, this 'pledge' was the part that really creeped Mallard out. It was the best he could do to vaguely mumble along...

* * *

A short time later, Art was inconspicuously trailing Master Overseer Therodrux through the corridors of the old, condemned school complex. It was a shadowy dump of a building that had gone up hastily in its day, only to be boarded shut with still greater haste. The story held that in his failing days, the late Czar had gone on diplomatic tour of Jast-Madiir's pitiful northern neighbor-state – Despotopia – only to come back with the distasteful revelation that its sooty, impoverished peasants were actually better-educated than his own. Unable to live with the thought of being outdistanced in anything by the favored punching-bag of the entire

Archipelago, the Czar rushed to cobble together educational facilities that could accommodate a reasonable percentage of urban children and teach them basic math and literacy and junk...

An afterthought from its inception, the unsightly school buildings themselves were about the only thing that came of the entire project. For when, just a few years later, the current Czarina took over management of the country, it wasn't long before she realized that her father's vision was economically foolhardy. At any rate, the idea of taking time that children might otherwise have spent generating capital and wasting it on strictly superfluous intellectual development failed to grab her. After all, there were already universities for the skilled trades... and according to Dronehood surveys, even in the boonies, literacy rates were about one in three... high enough for word of new laws and edicts to spread reliably. Surely that was enough. Public education thusly got the axe, and without so much as the time or money taken to properly tear the schools down...

Now, in secret, these schools were being used in a dark and twisted facsimile of their original purpose. It was not precisely education that was happening behind the boarded-up windows Art found himself passing sneakily by. *Re*-education was more like it...

He leaned his head round a corner in the halls, ears attentively trained. By now, he was pretty well convinced that this man Therodrux was his mark: the secret mastermind that kept the Digit Cults alive and healthy throughout the last dozen raids that were supposed to have ended their ilk for good. Every time the Inquisitors nabbed a ringleader, it turned out there was yet another, deeper ring in the infrastructure. The days of trying to nip the Cult in the bud had come and gone. It was going to have to be painstakingly pulled up by stubborn roots...

Art recoiled behind the bend as Therodrux checked over his shoulder. Huffing air to keep himself cool and collected, he privately darned his present lot. It turned out there were disadvantages to being a notoriously chic private eye, the biggest of which was getting roped into these dangerous high-stakes assignments. Spy work wasn't Art's flavor. There was a reason he'd labored so long and hard to learn how to be invisible. It was easier, he felt, than acting...

"Hi, Mart," he heard, and it made him jump. After a frantic mid-air search, he found Teresa to his left, looking up at him with rather confused but friendly eyes. She was a petite young Human the St. Argonsburg police had earmarked as a known Cultist. Art befriended her a few weeks ago under his fiendishly-clever assumed identity – *Mart Allard.* While not very inventive, it had the virtue of being close enough to his real name that he could respond to it instinctively. That made it much better than the random pseudonyms he'd tried in the past... crazy ones, such as 'Paul Hopper,' and 'William Drake'...

"Oh, uh, hi Teresa," Art replied, grasping internally for a cool cover-story to dismiss his present hunkering in a corner. "I was, er, looking for the bathroom."

Her brow knit, but she sort of laughed it off. "Is that what you were doing? It looked a bit like you were... I dunno... sneaking around..."

His heart skipped a beat. This little gal was too perceptive for his own good...

"Yeah, well, when you think about it, it's kind of embarrassing to have to go to the bathroom," he explained. "So I try to be inconspicuous."

She shrugged. "Okay." Then she turned and looked behind her. "Well, the plumbing was never actually hooked up. But I can show you the outhouses... back this other way."

Art just grinned. *Naturally,* she was going to lead him in exactly the wrong direction. His mission-critical eavesdropping would have to wait. "Oh, *this* way," he chuckled. "Right."

* * *

"So, what did you think of Professor Buelschestein's lecture today?" Teresa asked as they walked, sending Art's mind racing again for another slick lie...

"Are you kidding? It was the bee's knees," he answered. "The way he led-up to his point about those extra phalanges by starting *all* the way up at the collar bones? Pure genius! What a way to build suspense!" He sighed. "Lots, and lots, and *lots* of suspense."

She pointed at his face. "You've got crust in your eyes, you know."

He carefully flicked the gunk away, though it was too little, too late. "Heh, so I do! It was such an intense lecture, my eyes crusted over with zeal!"

For a while, they just walked in silence while Art fretted about the failing integrity of his false front. "Tell me, Mart..." Teresa said at length, clearly segueing to something else he wasn't prepared to answer, "...what was it that made you suspect the truth about thumbs in the first place? I mean, *something* must've happened."

"Nah, not really," Art waved it off. "If it's a story you're fishing for – a moment of epiphany – I don't really have one."

"All of us have a story," she insisted. "Come on. What's yours?"

"I dunno," he shrugged. "One day I just kind of looked at my hand, see? You know... *really* looked at it. And I thought, 'Hey, this one over here'..." he pointed at his own thumb, "...'this has *got* to be different.'"

She nodded rather absently. "Simple as that, huh? Just one good look, and you had it all figured out."

He studied her. "Is that so unusual?"

"It is to me." Her head hung. "I have to admit, I was a bit more skeptical. I needed... well... some convincing."

Ominous as that sounded, Art seized the opportunity to ask an investigatory question. "Who convinced you? Was it Master Overseer Therodrux? He really seems to know where his head's at! We're lucky to have him for a leader."

She shook her head. "But he's *not* the leader. There's someone else. Someone more... more elevated."

Art stopped in his tracks, eyes bulging. "*More* elevated than the *Supreme* Elevated Grand Master Overseer?!"

"If you'll believe it," Teresa answered meekly. "And you should. I can promise you he's very real. He's the one that showed me the *truth*."

Art whistled. "Sounds like a mighty persuasive fella."

While she met his gaze, the fear in her eyes steadily intensified. "You can't imagine. He has powers of persuasion... like I don't know how to explain."

They slowly started walking again; Art shook his head. "And here I was so set on meeting Therodrux." He volunteered a toothy, nervous grin. "I admit... I was sort of tailing him back there. But I guess I got star-struck, in the presence of such a visionary. Now you go and tell me there's someone even *he* answers to! Man, it'd sure be something to meet the Overseer's overseer..."

"I could arrange it, if you'd like," she informed him, a peculiar hesitance in her voice. Art stopped her again...

"No foolin'? You mean you can set up a meet-and-greet between little ol' me and the double-secret architect of the whole kit and kaboodle?"

She nodded. "Sure. Everyone in the Cult meets him eventually. One way or the other."

He patted her on the shoulder. "I gotta hand it to ya, sister... that is far out and groovy!" Then he clapped his enthusiasm. "Boy, I can hardly wait!"

"That's just as well. You won't have to wait long."

Reaching the end of a hall, Teresa pushed through a pair of double-doors, and they were suddenly standing in brilliant daylight. "There's the outhouses," she explained, pointing. "That is, if you really had to go at all."

"Well, now it comes to it, maybe a pitstop would be in order." He checked his timepiece. "Either way, it's high-time I buzzed out of here. Can't be late for work!"

"That's for sure," she assented. "We Cultists can't risk being indiscrete. Not yet."

"Right," he agreed. Then he gave her a thumbs-up and a wink. "Thanks for showing me to the little boys' room."

Suddenly, she got a wild look. She abruptly patted down his hand, checking around them like she was afraid who might be watching. "Oh, you mustn't do that, Mart," she told him.

His ears set as he tried to figure her. "What? No thumbs-up allowed?"

"*Decidedly* not. Not now, nor ever again... until the world is free from bondage to liars."

Art nodded with troubled solemnity. "Okeedoke."

Thoroughly creeped-out again, he defused the situation with another look at his pocket watch. "I really better get going. But thanks again... and not just for making sure I found the outhouse. I'm thrilled at the prospect of meeting our big kahuna. My future here's looking brighter and brighter all the time!"

She pursed her lips, suddenly avoiding eye contact. "There's no need to thank me. I brought you here in the first place. Whatever happens from now on is no favor. It's my responsibility."

* * *

After following through on a quick trip to the bathroom, Art Mallard made his way back up several tiers into the city of St. Argonsburg. It was a steamy day, but breezy, with all indications that the short break in the rainy season they'd been enjoying was about to end. Even so, Art was scarcely troubled by the humidity, or the thought of rain, or even the stark revolutionary overtures of the Digit Cult. He just climbed airily along the stairs and paths, keen on meeting his contact from the SAPD...

Soon enough, he was reclined in a wire-backed chair, sheltering under the umbrella at his bistro table beside The Yakety Crab, perusing their menu again with careful disinterest... he certainly didn't want to look at it so hard that no one could find him. It was around about the third time he reached the dessert section when the wide brim of a familiar hat appeared in view, just over the laminate. He set the menu down...

"Heya, Snookums," he greeted his officious law-enforcement liaison.

"Hello, Mr. Mallard." Blucille Cordon's voice was tired, but her grin belied her. "How did things go today?"

"All in good time," he replied, tapping the table. "Pull up a chair; take a load off. I'll tell ya all about it."

She looked around, sat a bit hesitantly. "Really, I'm... pressed for time. Much as I'd like to hang around and chat, it might have to wait until Friday."

"Friday?" Art repeated back to her with an amused smile. "You mean, the Friday we've already rescheduled eight different times?"

"Nine, actually."

"My point exactly. Come on, Blucille... kick up your heels for just a minute. Whatever mountain of work you've got to scale today, you'd be better off doing it with a little early lunch." He turned his head, catching sight of a waiter with a tray on a hopeful beeline. "Anyway, looks like you're just in time! Here it comes now."

She rolled her eyes at him. "I might've known you had ulterior motives for arranging our meeting at a restaurant. Though I didn't take you for a seafood man."

"It's not my favorite," Art admitted, even as the waiter set the entrée on the table. "But you can't beat the way they serve it here." The waiter removed the cloche from the platter as if on cue, revealing a pair of big, pale, yellowing salmon – heads disjointed away from empty guts, eyes glossed over by a milky fog. "Still smiling back up at ya."

Blucille nodded appreciatively. "I have to admit, presentation counts for something. And I *am* famished." She took the strap of her briefcase off her shoulder. "As long as you don't mind me doing a bit of paperwork on the side, I suppose I can make time..."

Art sighed dramatically... smirked sarcastically. "Well, if you must."

"I promise I'll only work on one file," she said, the contents of her case already lining the table. "You get an even 50% of my attention."

"More like 33, if you factor-in the eating." He nodded in a doting sort of way. "Still, it's an improvement."

Her pen started scratching away while she chewed on her fish like a big noodly drumstick. "Alright," she said between bites, "now let's have your report. Did you get anything on Therodrux?"

He shrugged. "Nothing new. All we've got is a name, a face, and a doozy of a title. Though, I suspect the name's no better than an alias anyway."

She nodded at her papers. "That was our thinking. Especially when the Dronehood couldn't turn up any record of a 'Therodrux Mengaloid'. Of course, whatever grandiose title he gave himself is no use either. If there was only a way you could give us his *face*, we might get somewhere."

Art reached into his vest pocket. "I *did* make a sketch, for what it's worth." He handed her the sheet of paper.

Once she'd hurriedly unfolded it, Blucille's eyes danced over a smiley-faced stick figure. "Not bad," she admitted. "Could almost pass for one of our professional sketches."

"Thanks. I really tried to capture the smugness."

She stuck the sketch away in her case. "Well, if push comes to shove, we'll post it. But honestly, Mallard, I hoped you'd come away with something more."

"I did," he assured her. "But you're not going to like it."

She shot him an exasperated look over her fish. "Okay. What else did you find out?"

"That Therodrux isn't our man."

She replaced both pen and fish to table. "Really?"

"Nope. Turns out there's another rung in the ladder: some shadowy puppet-master with an unnatural talent for persuasion."

Blucille sighed, sinking back in her seat as she refocused. "Alright then. So what do we know about *him*?"

"We know exactly zilch about squat with a side of zippo," Art explained. "No face, no name, no title. Nada."

"*Terrific*," she growled, huffily returning to food and work.

"...But I *am* going to meet him. Soon, I've been told..."

Her brow rose. "Well, that's different. And either way, I suppose you've done us a huge favor. We never suspected anyone above Therodrux."

"Yer welcome," Art nodded, doing a finger gun. "Though I confess, I still don't really understand how breaking up these Digit Cults ever came to rest on my shoulders. It shouldn't even be the SAPD's problem. Let the Inquisitors handle it, like they usually do..."

"They *have* been handling it," Blucille explained. "They've broken up the Cult over, and over, and over again... and every time it seems to grow back larger than before. Whoever this mystery-leader is has been too careful and too clever. The Inquisitors can't get close enough to the situation. They can't infiltrate. That's where you come in."

"That still doesn't explain *your* part in it," Art argued. "Surely the Inquisitors know how to hire an investigator. What turned this into police business?"

"The Cults did," she answered with a full mouth. "In addition to growing back ever stronger, they've also become more bold. Recently, they've gone so far as to issue a written ultimatum to the Czarina herself, demanding that she break ties with the Inquisition... even declare it a body of foreign usurpers and an enemy of the state. Failure to do so, they warned, would necessitate her forcible removal from office."

Art huffed. "I'll bet she liked *that*."

"And how. At any rate, that should be sufficient to explain our involvement."

"Sufficient, alright."

Blucille stopped short of taking another large hunk out of her salmon, giving Art a sudden quizzical look. "When were you planning on eating, anyway? You haven't even touched your fish yet..."

"Must've slipped my mind," he quipped. "I suppose I could at least start unrolling my napkin..."

Blucille froze again, blanching as his comment prompted her to stare wide-eyed at her silverware, still bound tight in facial tissue. *"Good grief,"* she breathed, turning her look on the shredded salmon in her hand. "All this time... I've been eating like a slob..."

"No sweat," Art assured her. "Food takes on a whole new beauty, when you're the one scarfing it."

She tore through the paper band and made a lightning-fast run along her jowls with her napkin. The tissue paper and her furry face concealed it, but he could swear she blushed. "You're such a huge dork."

"The dorkiest."

While he finally unsealed his own napkin and silverware, and they began civilized dining in synchronous, Blucille rejoined meaningful conversation. "How will you know when it's time to meet with your secret kingpin character?"

"I expect they'll get a hold of me in their own time," Art reasoned, fork and knife flaking fish. "That's how they arrange most of their confabs. Until they do, I'll have to stay in deep cover. Can't afford to blow the whole thing if they go looking for me 'on the job' and I'm not there."

"And what if they decide they want their meeting on *Friday*?" she verbally nudged him.

He pointed at her with his fork. "In that case, Darlin'... I'll make *them* reschedule."

She smiled. But after a moment, her face contorted with concern. "There *is* something I was supposed to relay to you: a message from Deborah Boulevard."

Art paused, his appetite suspended for the moment. "Let me guess... a *Code Capital - 'I'*?"

She nodded.

Art sighed. "Well, no surprise there. Knowing Horus, he was bound to take this latest case pretty hard." His eyes scanned empty air while he considered what to do. "I suppose I can get away tonight. Odds are pretty good the Cultists won't contact me right away."

"Probably best. If you go see him tonight, you won't be alone. I hear Blackforest has a big new job for him."

"Good deal," Art said, relieved to know it. "That at least stands a chance of cheering him up a bit."

The Assistant District Attorney checked her timepiece. She shot up out of her seat. "I have to go." In a blur of action, she had her papers wrangled and was wound up to take off like a rocket. But somehow, just before launch, she managed to pause and begrudge him a soft expression. "Good luck helping your friend. And for goodness' sake, remember to watch your back with those Cultists. They're more cunning than they seem."

"Don't worry your little head, Daffodil. Everything's gonna turn out fine." He gave her a cutesy wave goodbye. "See ya Friday."

She nodded. "Friday."

Chapter 3

The whistle blew a final, anguished moan as the train went careening into another abysmal tunnel through the bones of the mountain. On a tempestuous night, in the dregs of the late rainy season that heralded frigid winter, racing down subterranean paths that would never see the light of day, the mood was nothing if not... well... *moody*. Brakes screeched and screamed in the black echo-chamber, with slick wheels on slick tracks bearing thousands of tons of deadweight down the slopes of Mt. Norvein...

But to someone who made the circuit every night, all this gloom and clamor was no better than a discordant lullaby. It did nothing to dispel or otherwise disrupt Horus' already fitful slumber. While his body tried to rest, limply draped over his desk, his mind was far away, trapped back in court...

In his mind's eye, he watched himself as he stood...

"Your Honor," he called out. "I must protest the ruling of the court." He gestured to his left. "The body of evidence presented against this man has never strayed from the purely circumstantial. I beg an extension... a postponement of judgment..."

"The ruling of the Court is final," the judge said, filling the hazy room with his echoey voice. "And the defense will refrain from further appeals." A hideous grin curled across his face. "Besides, Templar, I do not see any *man*, there in the seat beside you..."

Horus was seized with a sudden, senseless dread. Where would the defendant be, if not in his seat? But the judge's assertion came on such an air of self-satisfaction. How could it be false?

Horus didn't want to see... didn't want to confirm the answer to this most unwanted riddle. He knew, somehow, *exactly* what he would see before he saw it...

It was all he could do to slowly – laboriously – force himself to turn and look. And sure enough, as his eyes strayed down, the sight that most terrified him was there to meet his gaze...

There truly *wasn't* any man next to him...

...It was just an empty chair...

"Horus," he heard: a distant melody beckoning to him from the waking world...

"No... the *chair*..." he muttered, unconscious.

"*Horus,*" he heard again, as he was shaken bodily by an unseen force...

"Someone has to sit in the chair!" he insisted, clinging to the dream for all he was worth, though it scourged him...

"Horus!" Deborah called for the third time. At last, Horus sat up straight, groggy eyes rallying their focus. After a few moments, he settled his look up at her...

"Yes, Deborah?" he asked hoarsely.

"You were having that nightmare about the empty chair again," she explained.

He ran his hand down his face. "So I was." He could remember it plainly, even now... and it was hardly any wonder. Like many of the very worst nightmares, this one had its basis in fact. Not much more than one insufferably long and miserable week ago, he *had* been representing what amounted to an empty chair... that is, an *absent client*... a man who'd allegedly jumped ship when he'd learned he was sailing for war. On the man's behalf, Horus had fought an agonizing legal battle, eclipsed only by an even more agonizing defeat... one his subconscious mind was clearly not prepared to let go of...

"I'm sorry if I disturbed you," he said at length, growing embarrassed. Deborah had either just made a spot-on guess... or he'd been sleep-talking. Had she heard him call out and come to his aid from all the way in her own office car?! That would indeed be humiliating...

"Well, to tell the truth, Boss," she began delicately, interlacing her fingers, "I *have* been a little concerned for you the last few days." She labored silently toward another point. "We *all* have."

Horus sighed. He knew from experience what *that* meant. He buttoned the top of his shirt and pulled his tie back into place...

"I assure you, the concern is misplaced. I'm really alright." He stood from his desk. "But now, I suppose I'll have to give the others the same assurance. They're already waiting for me in the next car, I presume?"

She shrugged apologetically. "Well, you know how it is. And after all, what's a friendly little kick in the pants, every so often?"

"Still a kick in the pants," he answered. "But never mind. Let's get this over with..."

"Yes, while we're still in the tunnel," she agreed. "It's a deluge out tonight."

Horus shrugged, opening the door to his office car. "When it rains, it pours." He gestured for her to go first, before he himself walked out into the wind and the howling, pulling the door closed behind him...

The door with the fine monograms...

Horus Templar – Public Defender

Sure enough, a sparse gathering of irritatingly anxious faces was waiting in ambush for him as they pushed into Deborah's office car. Horus reflexively tugged his collar up and his coat tails down, feeling an ironic sort of aloofness. Deep down, he knew they genuinely cared, and didn't seek his embarrassment. So much better, then, that he should seem very much unembarrassed...

"Hello, everyone," Horus said, looking over Art and Hamilton while Deborah made her way past her own cozy (almost cluttered) furnishings toward the far corner of her car. He spoke with self-reinforcing confidence, sure now that he could project a cool ease. "To what do I owe the pleasure of this impromptu little visit?"

Art shot up from his chair. "Horus, this is an intervention!" he announced.

Horus facepalmed, abruptly stonewalled. "Yes, I think I recognize your little charade by now. This isn't the first time." He coached himself to be cordial. "Look, I know I've been handed a tough loss. I know you're all aware how seriously I tend to take these *In Absentia* trials. I know that, historically, I've held onto the grief they've caused me longer than I should. But I promise you... *this* time, I'm really doing alright."

"Baloney," Art contested. "You've been dealing with all your old problems."

Horus' jowls curled a bit, like he wanted to show some teeth. But he metered his response. "That simply isn't true. I haven't..."

"...Deborah says you've been having those nightmares you always get," Art interjected.

Well, there was no denying *that*. He'd just been pulled from one...

"I suppose I've had a bad dream or two. But that's a perfectly ordinary..."

"...And you've been scarfing pure lard again when you think no one's looking!"

Horus blanched. He *did* have a bad habit of comfort-eating in times of crisis. But he rallied. Surely, they were just guessing. There was no way they'd found his stash this time...

"I most certainly have not! What on earth would make you think..."

Just then, they all seemed to turn and look in unison back at Deborah. She produced his secret tub of lard, holding it out with an accusatory expression while she stood by one of her windows...

"Well, alright... but never more than a spoonful at a time. It's really quite under control..."

Deborah opened her window, and held the tub out toward the funnel of rushing air...

"No, come on, now..." he protested, reflexively reaching. "Don't..."

Deborah flung the lard out into the void.

Horus hunched, a defeated man. His ears were hot as they folded back tight against his head. "Alright. I suppose I needed that."

Hamilton Blackforest gestured to an open chair. "Why don't you have a seat, Horus?"

Rather than bother with balking anymore, Horus silently obliged the District Attorney. In any other case, it might've been particularly humiliating to have the very nemesis who'd just defeated him present for such an occasion. But the two men knew each other very well... much too well for Horus to suspect Hamilton had come to gloat...

Once they were all sitting, Art leaned in aggressively. "Now listen here, Pal: enough's enough! You're just going to have to..."

"...Ah-ah! Hold it, Art! Just simmer-down!" Blackforest talked him down. "Let's hear what *he* has to say first. Let him get it all out... if that's possible."

All eyes were so intently fixed on Horus that it was very difficult not to wax agitated a second time. He'd just as soon sit in defiant silence. But he knew that would get nowhere. "Well, I doubt if I'll be able to express my displeasure any more eloquently than I've done before. It's the same with every *In Absentia* case. I can't help wondering how I might've helped the man better, if I only could have met him. *Talked* with him. Learned what really happened. But as it is, he may have simply fallen overboard in a moment of carelessness. He may've been washed away bodily by a rogue wave. He might've even been eaten right off the deck by a killer seahorse."

"There's no such thing as a killer seahorse," Art reminded him. "Not that we know of, anyway."

"No, and that's precisely my point," Horus argued. "There's so much we don't know... and can *never* know... without the defendant. Even if he'd only lied to me, we would've been more likely to learn *something* of the truth than with no statement at all. But why suspend judgment for the sake of accuracy?" he asked woefully. "The court passed down its best guess – based solely on circumstantial evidence – and called it justice."

Here, Blackforest waded into the conversation. "Alright. Suppose I go ahead and stipulate the possibility that *justice* might not have been served here. Would you at least concede that the *law* has its own terms of due process, which the trial satisfied?"

"I suppose. But law ought to *be* just... or, at the very least equitable. If one man is denied the right to be present for his own trial, then why should any man enjoy such a right?"

"'If a law is to be unfair, then let it be unfair to all'," Blackforest quoted. "Yes, we've all read your dissertation, Horus."

"Except me," Art put in. "Sorry, Buddy... it was kind of a snooze."

"I think we're all beginning to veer away from *the point*," Blackforest said through rows of razor-sharp teeth, angling a glare at Art.

"What point is that, Hamilton?" Horus asked. "I would be greatly consoled to have one."

Blackforest withdrew into the recesses of his chair, arms propped on their rests as he clicked his long nails together. "The point *I* want to make is this: You're obsessing over unanswerable questions. You're letting your fixation on ideals drive away your rationality. Tell me this, Horus: Even if your client *had* been present, and he could prove that he'd simply fallen into the ocean, or been eaten by a sea monster of some stripe or other, would *any* of that have been a satisfactory excuse for abandoning his post, under the law of the land?"

Horus closed his eyes, massaged the bridge of his nose. "No."

"And, if you're quite honest with yourself, wouldn't you have to admit it's *overwhelmingly* more likely that he did knowingly, and willfully, jump ship rather than face war in Despotopia?"

He sighed his exasperation. "Yes, that is the most likely explanation."

"Well, there you have it, then. The court *did* pass its best guess... nothing short of it. And the verdict would have been the same regardless."

"Not only that," Deborah put in, "but I think you need to give yourself some credit, Boss. You did your very best to cast reasonable doubt."

"Darn straight," Hamilton nodded.

"And you leveled some scalding arguments at *In Absentia* while you were at it," Deborah went on. "You fought your best fight, Horus. You went to bat for your client, and you challenged the inequity of the system. There's really nothing more you could've done. You'll just have to be content with that."

Horus managed to fix a weak grin on his face. "You're right, of course. Both of you. And I'm grateful. It should help me... in the waking hours." He looked off far away, then... rolling his fingers under his chin. "Now, if only I could find a way to sleep, without always coming up against that empty chair..."

At this juncture, Blackforest sighed. "Well, hopefully I've brought something that can help with that, too. Something for your mind to sink its teeth into... subconscious and all..."

Horus' ears perked. "A new client?"

"Yes... exactly," Blackforest said, a strange reservation in his voice. Horus was quick to inquire...

"Is something the matter, Hamilton?" he asked.

Blackforest sucked in a breath as he slowly produced a manilla folder from within his suit jacket. "You've had some odd cases this year already... this might not be the least of them." He locked eyes on Horus. "Moreover, you've got another client of... well... an exotic nature, shall we say?"

Horus almost chuckled. "Surely no more exotic than Aphelo was."

"Your bug-client?" Blackforest shook his head. "No, not quite. This one's of foreign stock, sure enough, but at least he hails from the civilized world. In recent millennia, anyway..." He got a steely look that signaled he was finally coming to the uncomfortable revelation he'd been holding back. "He's a Berlie Beirel, Horus."

Before Horus could formulate any sort of reaction, however dismissive, Art leapt back in. "Eh, how do you like that? A no-good home-wrecker."

Faintly did Art register the simultaneous, reflexive grunts that Deborah and Hamilton choked back. By now, he'd already stepped in it, and there was nothing they could say to help him...

"Don't do that," Horus cautioned him, backing it up with a look more unpleasant than any Art had ever seen contort his friend's features... least of all while he was looking at *him*...

"What?" Art asked, searching around as if to deflect the brunt of Horus' displeasure to some other target. "What did I do?"

"You know very well what you did... try to implicate an anonymous Berlie Beirel in age-old atrocities he had no part of."

Art just searched Horus for a while... stunned by his sudden vehemence, and hoping to ferret-out some trace of sarcasm. Fortunately, his expression of pained incredulity was enough to soften Horus. He turned to Blackforest...

"...That is, unless Hamilton here is about to tell me this fellow has been charged with some sort of domestic demolition?"

Blackforest cleared his throat as they all began to breathe again, seeing Horus had let the confrontational moment pass. "No, nothing like *that*. Perhaps you've heard: There's a shortage of Clerks these days, all across the Archipelago."

"Ah, yes," Horus nodded knowingly. "Depleted by the War. So, whose draft order has the Berlie Beirel in question elected to ignore? North or South?"

Blackforest chuckled nervously. "Whether you know it or not, you've arrived at the operative question. The answer is: *both*."

Horus tapped his chin in consideration. "Hm. Well, I support your conclusion, Hamilton. I begin to see the makings of another peculiar case."

"You bet your sweet dew claws." The DA shook his head. "Three nations, fighting over one drone..."

"*Three*?" Horus repeated. "Has the Tophthaeran Civil War really progressed to that? An official schism in the country?"

"Yes it has. After nearly seventy years of Tophthaeran envoys bogging the international courts down with appeals to recognize one Queen or other as *the* Queen, it seems the jellies have finally given up and shelved the whole effort. Irisa has restyled the northern isle of Tophthaera into Tophthera, and Asiri presides over the new sovereignty of southern Tophthaera, known as Toefthaera."

"You just said the same name like a zillion times," Art accused Blackforest.

In response, Hamilton reached into a pocket and retrieved a sticky note. "The spellings are all different," he explained, handing it off to Art. After a quick study of the note, Art could only shrug...

"*Oookay* then. I guess that counts..."

"It *does* count," Blackforest assured him. "The Annex Tribunal has already recognized both Tophthera and Toefthaera as independent claimants in this case. And in merely contesting their claims, our own justice department has followed suit. That pretty well makes them bonified nations, for all intents and purposes."

"If I might venture a shrewd question," Horus rejoined, "why *is* the justice department allowing itself to get tied up in all this intrigue?"

"Well, your client *is* a citizen here. That gives us a stake. And anyway, we really are running low on Clerks. The Czarina wants to stem that, if she can. If the workers get too few, she might have to conscript non-Meduselda to fill in the gaps. But that would mean paying some of the Clerks enough to live on."

"I see," Horus nodded. "That would seem to answer most of my questions out of the gate. But there is one caveat left you've been fairly dancing around, Hamilton."

"I was coming to it. Anyway, you will've reasoned the implications for yourself. An international caper like this means an international stage. You're being shipped-out, Horus. Your case is to be heard by the Tribunal itself... at the highest level."

Horus' brow rose. "A hearing with the Viziers," he said. "That is a somewhat daunting prospect."

"Hence the need for this whole friendly pep-talk," Blackforest explained, gesturing widely. "You're going to have to be at the top of your game, Horus. The Twin Queens have been trying a long time to get a case before the Viziers. I'd wager good money the prosecutors aren't going to take the fate of this one little drone lightly. They'll be coming ready for war."

Horus stood from his seat. "No doubt you're right. I'd do well to take my own war-council, in the morning." He forced a tired look... not a difficult thing to do, since he truly was exhausted. "Are we done here?"

His three compatriots shared glances before nodding.

"Very well," Horus said. "Thank you all again. I'm sure I feel much better now."

He pushed his way out the door, and into an icy torrent of swirling wind and rain...

Oh yes, he thought to himself. *So much better...*

* * *

Scarcely had Horus shook what water he could from his pelt, loosened his tie and replaced himself in the seat behind his desk for another merciless bout of sleeping, when suddenly his door came open. In walked Blackforest, his fur matted in sharp clumps by instantaneous drenching, his huge fangs exposed as he gritted through the chill. In such a bedraggled state, he appeared more prepared to ferally rend people and things in pieces than Horus had ever seen him, aside for the sorrowful look that crept into his eyes...

"Something more, Hamilton?" Horus asked.

"Yes," he replied, dripping by the door.

Horus gestured. "Don't hesitate to have a seat."

"No, I think I'll just keep it brief." After announcing his brevity, he paused for some moments while the water ran down, evidently at a loss. "I did mean to... *apologize*... for sticking you with a Berlie Beirel for a client. I want you to know: It was really out of my hands."

Horus couldn't help adopting a sour countenance in that moment. Art hadn't known any better than to say what he said about Berlie Beirels. What was Blackforest's excuse? "Frankly, Hamilton, your sympathy is misplaced. It makes no difference to me at all that he's a Berlie Beirel."

"Don't forget who you're talking to, now," Blackforest cautioned, pointing Horus down. "You and I go pretty far back, Horus. Don't you think I know you better than that?"

Horus only darkened, beginning to feel like he was being deliberately provoked. "If you think the fact of his heritage offends me, I'd say you don't know me very well at all."

Blackforest shook his head. "It's not *that*."

"Then *what*?" Horus demanded, while he waited impatiently for the DA to explain himself.

"Well I *just*..." he started angrily, before abruptly collecting himself and softening again. "I know how it would tend to remind you of, well, some of the darker chapters of your own past. That's drama you don't particularly need right now. I would've spared you from it, if I could have."

Horus' indignation finally abated, seeing Blackforest's heart was really in the right place. He stood back up, rather than perpetuate the discourtesy of being the only one sitting. "Well, in that case, I thank you. But you know how it goes. The demands of work aren't always easy or comfortable. We all have to take the bad with the good."

Blackforest nodded. "That's a fine truism."

"Anyway, it's a long time since I made my peace with the 'drama' you're referring to," Horus went on. "I don't consider this case a nuisance. More like a unique opportunity... to prove the past really *is* all water under the bridge."

The DA shook his head with a sort of mocking smile. "You're always out to prove something or other, aren't you? If you're interested in my advice – I'm sure you're not – I'd say give it a rest for once. Just work the case and leave the idealism out of it."

Horus' brow knit. "Why should I do that?"

"Because whether you'll admit it or not, this is still a sore spot for you. That much is obvious. You're not as clear-headed as you might be. That's why I say: Keep it simple. Do your job. Focus on the law. That's the best thing you can do here."

"An interesting assessment," Horus replied, undaunted. "Any other kernels of advice?"

"Ha!" Blackforest force-laughed. "Where to even begin?" He took a moment to assess his old foil. "I suppose you might try being less of a heroic loner all the time... always trying to pretend things don't bother you, when they really do. You were never any good at pretending anyway."

"I think I know where to get support, if I need it," Horus argued.

"Says the man who's been secretly binge-eating pure lard," Blackforest countered.

Horus rubbed the back of his neck uncomfortably. "Well, let's just say you *reminded* me where I can get support."

"I hope so," Blackforest replied, a bit more stern. "I hope you don't soon forget again: There are good people who care about you. That Deborah... she's a real gem, Horus. I wonder if you know how fortunate you are to have her in your corner. And Art... well..." he hesitated. "I'm sure he means well."

Horus sighed. "You're right, of course. A man couldn't ask for better friends. I don't know why I often keep them at arm's length." After a moment of somber reflection, he looked wide about the room, as if to call attention to their presence in it. "Are you sure there isn't a third name you could put on that list of well-meaning good friends?"

Blackforest huffed. "None comes to mind."

As the conversation came to an impasse, both men started a search for segues to excuse themselves.

"Well, it *is* getting late, Horus," Blackforest announced finally, referring to his pocket watch. "Or actually, it's getting *early*. You should rest, and I have other heavy chores to get back to."

"When do I sail for the Tribunal?" Horus asked.

"I suppose I forgot to tell you that. Your boat leaves tomorrow, of course."

Horus nodded. "Naturally."

Blackforest made for the door, cursing under his breath when he reached the handle, remembering what a gale it was outside. "All the more reason to get some sleep," he called back. Then he turned, giving Horus a last look of solidarity. "And don't let any visions of an empty chair trouble you. You're not alone in this."

Chapter 4

Despite all Hamilton Blackforest could say, the dark hours that remained simply refused to pass quietly. Horus woke again with the night terrors before the end of the last pre-dawn circuit. Unable to return to sleep a third time, but too exhausted to bother waking up properly, he rode out the rest of the trip in a heap with his eyes shut. When finally, the train did stop, he scraped himself up off his desk, resolving to make up for lost rest by guzzling a hardy breakfast. He drank all of two ankylosaur eggs, removed his shirt, ran a brush over his onyx coat, and changed into a fresh suit. By the time Deborah and he had taken their first few steps in the cool, damp morning air, he felt passably refreshed... even energized at the thought of a new case waiting for him in a mysterious land across the Farjean Sea. A little change of scenery might be just the thing to cure his ails...

"How do you like finding out in the middle of the night that you're sailing for Roemnar in the morning?" Deborah asked on the road. "For me it's still a bit surreal. I can safely say I've never been."

"Most people haven't," Horus replied.

"It's a funny sort of a place to set up the highest court in the region," she went on. "Stick the isolationist country with all the heavy international cases! Whose idea was that?"

"Most likely it came down to simple pragmatism. Roemnar *is* the most central land in Idriulthoronta." He looked far ahead of them, musing. "And anyway, I think it's sort of fitting. If a single country must host the international courts, why not the one that has the least vested interest in international affairs?"

"Well, when you put it that way," Deborah sighed her agreement.

"Another thing that helps: They keep it tucked away on Vathiiki, their small satellite island. That's where they handle most of their business with other countries. Trade markets... foreign embassies. They're all to be found there, conveniently out of sight and out of mind from the vast majority of the Heron population."

"It's so nice to know when you're welcome," Deborah quipped. "But I suppose that explains why we're crossing over in a trade ship."

"Apparently you know our itinerary better than I do." He grinned at her. "Not that I should be surprised."

"You mean, you didn't ask Blackforest how we'd be getting around?"

Horus shrugged. "It escaped me. Anyway, I trusted him to have it all worked out by the time we came around to pick up my client."

"Ah yes, your client: *Mobipetrolluck*. We've got another jaw-breaker on our hands, Boss."

He blinked. "Is *that* his name?"

"Yes," Deborah confirmed. "What... you didn't get that from Blackforest either?"

"It seems all sorts of things escaped me a few hours ago," Horus admitted, rubbing the back of his neck. If nothing else, he should've thought to ask the drone's *name*...

"Well, you'd better focus-up," she nudged him. "We're headed for the big leagues now."

* * *

The morning that followed was to be a relentless series of meetings and partings. First of all, to their surprise, they crossed paths with Art Mallard, just about the time the Civil HQ building came into view...

"Good morning, stranger," Deborah greeted him. "You're up bright and early today."

"No problem, Debs," Art replied. "This isn't one of my sleeping days anyway."

She gave him a quizzical look. "*Debs*? That's new. Fresh out of proper pet-names, are we?"

He shrugged. "They *are* in short supply. Anymore I have to save the good ones for my little Googly Gumdrop."

"Well, how about that?" Horus put in, shaking his head. "I think we've both been downgraded, Deborah."

"How's that?" Art asked.

"It appears to me you've already paid your visit to the Station, with no thought of hanging around to bid us farewell on our voyage."

Art stood bug-eyed in front of them, momentarily at a loss for words. "Alright, you got me," he admitted. "I got the idea to come around and see my Sweet-Potatah Parsnip one more time before I spend the next few days in deep cover."

"What a sentimentalist," Deborah goaded him. "I'll bet that idea annoyed your Sweet-Potato Parsnip."

"Thoroughly," Art nodded. "She doesn't like me taking these kinds of chances while I'm undercover... being seen around the Station, and all. But ya know... I figure they're just a bunch of clueless fanatics anyway. So what's the harm?"

Horus looked over at Deborah. "I've got this whole thing backwards. It's we who should be wishing *Art* the best of luck." He turned, reached out and shook Art's hand. "Creatorspeed, my friend. Be careful. And, do try not to forget about us entirely before we get back."

"I'll give it my best shot," Art nodded. He winked at Deborah. "See ya 'round, Debs."

"Too-da-loo," she replied.

* * *

The next face of note along their journey was Blackforest's. He had a very impatient look about him, tapping his small shoe on the ground with arms folded, timepiece handy in one clawed fist. Horus wondered about this at once. Perhaps in his many oversights the night before, he'd also managed to mess up the time... perhaps they were *late*. He dismissed the idea at once: Deborah would never allow that to happen. No, as they engaged the DA, it became clear immediately that they were not the cause of his discomfiture. He was waiting on someone else...

"Good morning Horus, Deborah," he acknowledged them quietly, when at last he noticed them. He waved a policeman over. "Sergeant Huxley, would you mind showing Mr. Templar here to his client?"

The man Huxley nodded silently, signaling for Horus to follow him. Deborah automatically turned to go along, but Blackforest stopped her...

"Not you, Deborah," he said. "That is, if Horus can spare you a moment. There's another dimension of this trip to Roemnar I'd like to bring you up to speed on, now that it's all been arranged." He checked his watch. "*Hopefully*, anyway."

Deborah and Horus exchanged an anxious look, both quite without a clue what 'other dimension' Hamilton might be alluding to. "Okay," Deborah said at length. "See you in a few, Boss."

Horus nodded. "Yes... I'll be back presently." He allowed himself to be led away...

* * *

While their footsteps echoed through the hollows of the detention area, Horus steadied himself, dismissing all question of this mysterious development that was so troubling Hamilton. He would learn about it soon enough from Deborah, if not the District Attorney himself. Right now, he needed to put on diplomacy. He needed to be at his most engaged and cordial. From the very first, it had to be unspoken but understood that the ancient grudge between Mesomelae and Berlie Beirels was a non-issue... forgiven and forgotten... quintessentially, 'incompetent, irrelevant, and immaterial.' His client should enjoy that assurance. Moreover, the world at large should have just such an example...

Rounding a final corner, Horus caught sight of the drone, all a dull blue under white-and-black stripes as he hovered in his cell. Seeing the Berlie Beirel, he flushed his heart with all the easy non-hatred he had in his stores... and smiled with great, shunted sincerity...

"Hello, Sir," he said. "Allow me to introduce myself. My name is Horus Templar; I'm your attorney."

The Meduseldan inmate flashed with sudden alarm. "*Upon me word*," he said. "You're... you're a Mesomela."

Horus felt the slightest flash of annoyance, confronted all at once with *this* trifling detail about himself... out of all trifling details. "Yes," he nodded slowly. "That's true."

"Oh, blimey, but of course it is, Sir! Of course it is!" the drone waved urgently. "And you must pardon my bit of foolscap. I've never 'ad legal dealin's in me life. You caught me off guard, you did, is all. An' now I'm bound to be sore about it. Right sore indeed, that I didn't 'ave a proper apology prepared and waitin' when you arrived, Sir." He sighed, slouching heavy in the air with guilt. "I hope it's enough you know... I *am* sorry. *Very* sorry... for what I did to your people."

Horus was aware that he faintly twitched.

Not wanting to be at all ungracious to his client, he did his best to take the comment in stride. Hurriedly, he shrugged it off. "I'm sure I don't know what you're talking about," he said. He bit down on his own jowl, realizing his misstep too late...

"Oh, but surely you're aware, Sir! Of my Dominion's rather boorish behavior under Queen Aedeloma, some generations back now. We made war on the 'ole world, we did. And we sacked your people's countries and drove the lot of you into exile." He gestured to Horus with empty, upturned tentacles, ready to beg his final, heartfelt appeal for understanding. "Sorry 'bout that."

Now, Horus really had to strain to maintain composure. He cleared his throat. "I... *suppose* I should be grateful for your sentiments. However, I can't help noting that you are referring to events from hardly less than 5000 years ago... events neither you nor I could possibly have had any part in. And, as the alleged injured party, I would be remiss if I didn't convey my aversion to the idea that any man should express personal remorse for crimes that are not his own."

"Right you are Sir, of course," the drone prattled on with still more remorse. "Please don't take it personal-like, Sir, if it displeases you. Why not frame it more as *my* ancestors relaying their apologies to *your* ancestors? Surely something of that nature's in order..."

Horus looked about them, indicating the absence of said parties. "That would seem hyperbolic at best," he said. "Your only ancestors are the Queens... of which, only Aedeloma was truly villainous." He slumped a bit, resolving to share a bit of sensitive family history, if only it would diffuse the present mess. "And as for my *personal* ancestry, they were dealt a great deal less damage by her campaign than you suppose." He had to screw himself up a bit more, just to continue. "At the first sign of war, they fled for the coast. They rode out the worst of the 770 Years War tucked away in some quiet little corner of the world, when the rest of their countrymen chose to stay and fight. So now you see, no such apology is possible... or even warranted."

"I see Sir... I see," the drone replied, his voice still hesitant. "But even reckoning all those details... it doesn't seem to 'elp the matter, Sir. It doesn't excuse the undeniable fact that... well..." he struggled for the right words, "...people who superficially resemble me once did 'arm to people who superficially resemble you. An' I can't 'elp feeling that makes me a terrible person."

Horus just stood and blinked. Court was days away from convening, and yet his own trials were already in full swing. Despite his utmost goodwill, he couldn't seem to circumvent this whole meaningless impasse...

Finally, he put up his hands. "I don't know what more to tell you. I commend the fact that you have a conscience, even if it's quite misplaced. And you may rest assured that I don't hold history against you. I *will* represent you to the best of my ability in the coming days, Mr..." Horus blanched, coming up blank. "...Remind me what your name was, again?"

At last, a bit of life flashed into the dejected drone. "Mobipetrolluck, Sir, an' glad to make your acquaintance, such as I am."

"Mobipetrolluck," Horus repeated, nodding. "A good name... though it's long enough to be Despotopian. Is there anything people call you for short?"

"There is, Sir! Friends call me Lucky."

"Hm..." Horus said, catching some chin hair between his fingers as he pondered. "Given your present debacle, that seems rather inappropriate. How about I just call you 'Mo' instead?"

'Mo' bobbed his assent. "I'd like that, Sir, yes... it suits me fine."

Horus managed a grin. "Good." He clasped his hands together for sake of segue. "Now, I'm given to understand that you've been charged with draft evasion... by not one, but *both* Queens."

"It's all true, Sir... every word," Mo sighed. "I'm a lousy draft-dodger, twice over."

"I see," Horus said, searching the middle distance. "Well, that answers any question of your guilt... save one very important one. Whose summons came first? Was it Irisa's or Asiri's? If nothing else, I should be able to get you off *one* charge – I'd like to believe – if I could learn that much..."

Mo shook himself in denial. "But that's just it, Sir... *I don't know*. Honest, I don't. They both came in the mail on the same day..."

Horus' brow rose. This was shaping-up to be another proper head-scratcher. "That certainly complicates things."

"What *is* to be done with me, Sir?" Mo asked in his bewilderment. "Do you know? 'Ave you any guess?"

Horus shook his head. "Not the foggiest, I'm afraid. Not at present. Perhaps the mystery of the simultaneous summons can work in our favor. If the Tophtheran and Toefthaeran prosecutors find themselves deadlocked, the Tribunal might just be persuaded to uphold your residence here. I understand you're a Jast-Madiiran citizen..."

"That I am, Sir, yes! I filled out most every citizenship form you can think of in my time... even some for countries that 'aven't been around for ages! Chalk it up to personal indulgence. True, lots o' places rejected my applications... seein' as I'd never even been there. But Jast-Madiir took me up quick enough. I've lived and worked 'ere most of me life."

"That might help, too. At any rate, it gives me more grounds for contention than if you were only here on work visa. But don't get your hopes up too high. This is a very unusual case... unprecedented. I'll be spending the next few days brushing-up on international law. And I'll see what can be done about making your captivity as comfortable as possible, once we reach Roemnar."

"Comfortable?" Mo asked, quite perplexed. "I'm not sure I follow."

"Well, never mind," Horus replied. "As a non-violent criminal in a neutral land, I think you might be permitted certain leniencies. But there's no use saying more than that before I can be sure. I just need you to know: I have your best interests in mind."

"Right," Mo laughed nervously. "Very good, Sir... my thanks to you."

"I'm merely doing my job. You'll never have any need to thank me." He angled a look at the Clerk, hoping to make one last thing perfectly clear. "And, *certainly*, no further need to apologize." He nodded and turned to go...

"Sorry," Mo excused himself. Horus knew it was only a reflex. Still, it caused him a final shiver, as he hurried himself away...

* * *

By the time Horus returned to the lobby, he could see that Blackforest had progressed from brooding to fuming. Some of his unease had clearly passed to Deborah, as well. But she was quick to notice Horus' arrival, and carry on in her informal fashion...

"Well, that was quick," she called. "What do you think, Boss? Is this going to be an open-and-shut case?"

"That wouldn't be my guess," Horus replied, reaching them. "We're already running into some interesting complications. But there was little I could ask him at this stage that would avail much. A very brief meeting sufficed." Horus studied Blackforest, whose gaze was still far off. "When will he be transferred to the ship?"

"Soon," Blackforest answered, averting his eyes from a lateral survey only to check his watch again. "Perhaps *too* soon. Where the devil is Stenya? I swear, if he's had another episode, it'd better be his last..."

Horus gave up on Hamilton and turned to Deborah. "Something up with the Deputy Constable?"

She nodded gravely. "Blackforest just brought me up to speed. They're sending him along with us. He's had another spell with his heart. A very bad one this time."

Horus stroked his whiskers. "That's awful. But why put him on the boat to Roemnar?"

She looked away uncomfortably. "It seems his attending physician had her beak in a medical journal recently that suggested a promising new treatment for his condition. Purely in the experimental phase."

"His attending physician?" Horus asked, though it all quickly added up. "Yes, of course. I can only infer that means..."

"Oh yes," Deborah interjected. "We're bringing a Plague Doctor with us to plague doctor country."

"If they ever show up, you are," Hamilton put in, more privy to their sidebar than they'd guessed. "Blast it, if he's not here in the next *minute*..."

"But here they are now," Horus announced, pointing down the opposite corridor. Sure enough, another sergeant was wheeling Stenya Miloje along in an invalid's chair, while Doctor Nokkaeru strode abreast, keeping a dubious honor guard.

"Good morning, friends and associates," Miloje called to them.

"Good morning, Milo," Horus replied. "I'm very glad to hear you call it such."

"Why shouldn't I?" the stricken policeman asked as he was rolled into their midst. "I've had a new lease on life, of late... like every moment is illicit bounty, recaptured from the very jaws of death. How it makes the daylight to shine all the more bright... or some such nonsense."

"Do I detect a twinge of sarcasm?" Horus asked.

"Maybe a pinch," Miloje admitted, turning a sour face to Blackforest. "By all rights, they should be wheeling me out to the firing squad, rather than sending me on a cruise. That is what's traditionally done with a man who fails in his duties."

"We've been through this already, Stenya," Blackforest argued through clenched teeth. "You didn't fail at anything. You went out to collect a suspect, and you returned with him."

"There you go again, twisting the facts. I did *not* return with your suspect. *He* returned with *me*."

Blackforest twitched, his face all a big smile, bristling with insincerity. "I'm in no mood to stand here and argue the specifics of who brought in whom. You're both *here*. That fulfills your mission parameters."

Miloje pointed up defiantly. "That doesn't begin to excuse all that I'm not doing *now*. I should be heading this department. Instead I'm being carted about like so much baggage."

"You're training your replacement. That's another thing you're *supposed* to be doing. How better to train him than to throw him right into the thick of things and see if he sinks or swims?"

"Hmph," Miloje protested. "Some training. Unplanned. Unscheduled. I won't even be here to offer guidance, when he starts to slip up..."

"You let *him* worry about that. Just see that you make it back here alive and well. I'll be expecting your critique of his performance on my desk, the next day."

"You'll have it... on one condition."

Blackforest trained his ears. "What's that?"

"Do me a favor, Mr. Blackforest... and don't do me any more favors."

"I'll be very sure not to," he assured him. Then he looked up at the sergeant. "Sergeant Tarkinov, kindly see the Deputy Constable to the docks."

Tarkinov nodded and proceeded immediately. Horus hoped the Doctor would continue on with her patient silently. But of course, she lingered...

"How nice that we shall be travelling together, Counselor," she said to Horus. "I expect to enjoy it greatly. Already, you seem rather frazzled."

"Tired, is all," Horus fibbed. "It is... *nice* to see you," he lied outright. "All the more, knowing that you've found a hope for our dear Mr. Miloje." At least in this, he managed to inject some truth into their exchange...

"Hardly better than a shadow of a hope," she explained. "Even his candidacy as an outpatient is in question. But we will see about all of that soon enough." She turned her beak up under her horrible mask as she began again on her way. "In the meantime, you are encouraged to worry. Worry as much as you may... for all the good it will do him..."

"Bleah," Deborah quietly shuddered behind her back, summing up Horus' own feelings on the matter.

"Well said," Blackforest himself quipped. "But don't let her fool you. She'll see that stubborn old badger through this thing, if anybody can." He looked seriously at Horus. "You'd better fall in step yourself, Councilor. The boat won't wait for him. It might not wait for you, either."

"Might not?" Horus repeated, finding the DA's exact word choice a bit puzzling. He knew better than to think Hamilton would cast any doubt without purpose...

"I tried to tell you last night... you've been assigned to this case at a pretty high level, Horus... someone a few pay grades above me."

Horus grimaced. “So you *were* saying. ‘Out of my hands,’ you said. Well, what’s the riddle, Hamilton? Who’s pulling the long strings?”

“The order on my desk came down from the Czarina’s Chairman of the Trade Office.”

Horus’ face crumpled all the more. “The Trade Office? That’s crossing some disparate jurisdictions. What possible interest do they have in me?”

Blackforest threw up his hands. “You got me, Pal. All I have is the order...”

Chapter 5

Art watched precious beads of cool water splash down into the dirt from his tongue as he brushed his broom back and forth against the street. He could almost swear his well-tuned ears registered a faint simmering sound as each drop hit the hot granules. When the day began, he and his fellow street-sweepers achieved little more than whisking mud around, the ground still saturated from the night before. But the day had since progressed into a late scorcher, with broad daylight sapping the moisture out of everything but the oppressively humid atmosphere. A dry heat might've been nice... comfortable, even. But tropical Jast-Madiir seldom handed out such favors. Art wished he'd been granted an alias with a more comfortably cerebral job. Of course, that would've made for a trickier cover-story. It was easy enough to pretend like he knew his business, when all he had to do was brush the ground. Or, so he'd thought when he started...

"Hey, Mart!" Leroy scolded him. "Stop wasting all your time sweeping the dirt! You'll never get all the dirt out of the road."

"I should hope not," Art replied. "This is a *dirt road*." While he watched the brown earth turn ever paler shades of tan before his very eyes, he arrived at a novel question. "Why the Heck are we even sweeping this road, anyway?"

"Same reason we sweep every road in the city, you nitwit," Leroy answered. "To get rid of the *sand*!"

Art huffed. "*Sand... dirt...* tomato-tomáto! You expect me to believe there's a difference? Nothin'-doin', Buster."

Leroy just shook his head and went back to his own sweeping. "*Rookies...*" he muttered.

For his own part, Art also trained himself the more to his task. He didn't give a lick whether he was accomplishing anything or not, but he needed to look engaged. Anyway, he didn't benefit from letting his attention wander. Always he'd circle back to watching his fellow workers with envy, each one removing his construction helmet by sheer reflex over and over again to wipe his brow. In such a clime, Art could only be jealous of the Humans for being so leaky all over. One little drippy tongue was surely no ventilation system at all by comparison...

While such resentment turned over in his head for the umpteenth time, he only dimly registered another man from the team sweeping his way into closer orbit…

"Fine day, Mart," the man said at length.

Art felt a prickle of anxiety. His instincts and a bit of experience told him this had to do with his *real* reason for being here. "Yeah," he agreed cordially.

"Beats last night, anyway," the man went on.

Art kept sweeping. "What happened last night?"

"Had a rough game of darts. Only got one out of five."

Art swallowed a bit of his sweat-spit. His instinct was right. The man had just used their safe-phrase: *'One out of five'*…

Art checked and saw that no one else was nearby. "Out of five, one," he recited back, properly completing the exchange.

The man made one more quick, subtle survey of their surroundings before he continued in hushed tones, each of them still apparently engrossed in their sweeping. "The time is set, Mart. He wants to meet you tonight."

Art nodded without looking up. "Where?"

"Go to the school building, like usual," the man explained. "Master Overseer Therodrux will take you from there."

"Why not just tell me where to go? Can't they trust me to get where I'm going on my own?"

"He's a sight more cautious than that, Mart. And from what I've seen, he should be."

Art pushed through another wave of anxiety. "How do you figure?"

"That little quip about sand and dirt a minute ago," the man reminded him. "A true believer respects the difference in things. I'm not sure about you, Mart. But that'll be cured soon enough."

"You betcha, it will," Art agreed. "Once your mystery-leader gets a load o' me, there won't be any room left for doubt."

Though his eyes stayed down, Art could *feel* the man grin smugly. "I'm sure you're right about that."

* * *

Art had the rest of the day to juggle second thoughts and brooding. Was his façade really so weak that even Joe Cultist on the street doubted his convictions? That was not a good sign. The idea of being redirected to his final destination was far from comfortable, as well. The coppers already knew about the school building. If the Cult double-crossed him there, the SAPD would know right where to find him... or, at worst, they'd know where to find his body. Now he faced the possibility of disappearing completely, and accomplishing nothing. It was all enough to make a guy who was already used to looking at the glass half-empty feel almost too dumpy to stand...

In the end, though, he toughed it out. After his shift, he made for the school... waited for hours just inside the front door. And, by the time he'd nearly paced a hole in the floor, along came Therodrux, as promised. It was some small relief that things were finally going according to script. Better yet, the Master Overseer greeted him with obvious joy and exuberance... a far cry from the plain-spoken reservations of the man from his work detail. That also served to encourage Art. Maybe 'Joe Cultist' had just been unusually perceptive... a lone thinker in a crop of flunkies. Yes, how silly of him to forget so suddenly and so completely how dense these Cultists actually were. 'Mart Allard' might not go down as the best assumed identity of all time, but it was plenty good enough to fool the crazy thumb people...

That was when things started to take another bad turn...

After a brief, pleasant exchange with Therodrux, another couple of Humans pushed through the creaky metal doors of the school, casting long evening shadows with their big, muscly bodies.

"Hey there, guys," Art said, feeling obliged to acknowledge them, after they'd spent some long seconds staring him down. Of course, they were Humans, and not *quite* as big and strong as he was... but the margin wasn't as wide as he might've liked, and they had numbers on their side. "You coming to meet the secret leader, too?"

"Oh, they *are* coming," Therodrux answered for them. "But not for quite the same reason. You're a big fellow, Mart. I knew I'd need help transporting you."

Art laughed nervously, taking an involuntary step back. "I'm sure I can get there on my own power, wherever we're going. I'm tired from a long day's work, but nowhere near *that* tired."

The men encircled him like pack animals... a rather ironic role-reversal, Art managed to note. "You *could*, of course," Therodrux replied. "But I'm afraid that's not how we do things. Besides, Mr. Allard... you're looking more tired than you let on."

Art didn't get a chance to reply before one of the thugs reached out and chloroformed him. There were only a few muffled nothings, a feeling of weightlessness, and then, utter, black oblivion...

* * *

When Mallard eventually came-to, he couldn't help looking on the world with a fast-blinking confusion. He was in a bright room... well furnished, he saw, as his eyes began to adjust. A feral fear seized him as his emotions rushed to pick up where they'd left off. But where *had* he left off? He struggled momentarily to remember. He recalled a conversation with Therodrux... the arrival of big, nasty bruisers, and that suffocating sweet smell that knocked him right out of his socks...

He tried to reconcile this with his present condition. Everything was calm and nice. He was seated in a very comfy recliner, neither bound nor gagged. The bruisers were conspicuously (and welcomely) absent. The only thing that connected-up was that Therodrux was still with him. Art found the Overseer sitting across the room in another terrific chair, backed by a sparse bookshelf. As Art studied him, he just went on sitting... grinning... so motionless as to seem vacant. But finally, he spoke...

"Welcome, Mart Allard," Therodrux said.

Art took another look around, trying to figure things out all over again and maybe have them come out making sense. "Where am I?" he asked reflexively.

"That's not for me to say," Therodrux answered. "It is a secret place to all but the most devout. But you may call it The Bishop's Sanctum."

Art's brow knit. "*The Bishop's Sanctum*? Is that really the best you could do?"

"It's a name we're workshopping at present," Therodrux admitted.

"Fair enough." He worked to rub some of the haze out from between his eyes. "I guess the next question should be: Where's the *Bishop*?"

"Otherwise detained. He'll be along soon."

"Good," Art sighed. "This's all been a little too melodrama for my taste. I'd just like to meet the guy, profess the eternal truth of the thumb-as-digit, and get back to regular-old cultist life, if it's all the same to you."

Therodrux shrugged widely. "It makes little difference to me. But we'll have to see what *he* thinks. In the meantime, please be comfortable."

"*Right*," Art snarked, checking his timepiece.

* * *

Sitting there, under the silent observation of Overseer Therodrux, Art chanced many more occasions to refer back to his pocket watch. An hour oozed by. Two hours. All the while, Therodrux just sat there looking pleased with himself. It was easily the most uncomfortable time of Art's life. He didn't risk further conversation with the Overseer... his cover already seemed too strained. If Therodrux was only too happy to wait up for his boss like a vegetable, then it was probably best if Art followed suit. So, he painted a smile on – cramping most of his face muscles to keep some semblance of it there for the duration – while he busied himself drumming his cushy armrests with his fingers, snagging his nails countless times. Through it all, the pocket watch remained his only diversion. He checked it *again*...

At last, nearly on the mark of 14 past midnight, Overseer Therodrux stood up straight to no apparent cue. Timepiece still in-hand, Art did the same. He watched as a faint blue light was cast through the window of the door to the inner sanctum. It grew and throbbed and pulsed in a familiar rhythm he couldn't place. He should've been able to hear footsteps through the door, but he heard nothing. Testing the air, he *smelled* nothing. It was a maddening sort of mystery he had no time to unravel. The Bishop was *here*. Or, was he?

In the next moment, the door handle turned, and he had his answers... though they fell very short of dispelling his perplexity at it all. The Bishop came floating gently in, draped all in thick, dark layers of cloak. He was crowned with an impossibly tall collar that would've been more than sufficient to conceal his head, if he'd had one. He lofted over to the coat rack and removed a black vestment, only to reveal an even blacker one underneath. Then, knitting a pair of tentacles behind his back with a flourish of coat tails, he turned to meet his guest...

"Hello, my *child*," the Bishop called, his voice expressionless, soft like a whisper, but prickling with presence and power... and perhaps a hint of sarcasm. "We meet at last."

Art coached himself through a weak wave. "Howdy."

The Bishop flashed brightly while they considered each other. "Reservation. Apprehension. A confounded look. Is there something about me that surprises you?"

Art stared on, unblinking. "You're Meduseldan."

"Yes," the Bishop agreed. "Is that really so remarkable?"

Art shrugged. "I guess... well... I just figured the Bishop of the Digit Cults would be somebody with... you know... actual *digits*."

The Bishop raised and studied one of his own spade-shaped tentacle-ends. "And why should that be of any consequence? The truth is no less true, whether or not it pertains to me." He returned his tentacle and floated in closer. "But surely, a man like you won't be content to know me as 'the Bishop'. My name is Sabracore. That *is* what you came for... isn't it?"

"Sabracore," Art repeated, snapping with recognition. "A strong Wuu Gappew name, if ever I've heard one! That explains..." he caught himself. This easily qualified as a situation where it would be mildly indelicate to point out that Wuu Gappews were renowned the world over as the most impressionable and downright gullible of all the saps and suckers in history. If any Meduseldan could become so fixated on the idea that a thumb is not a finger as to start a fanatical insurrection over it, it would *have to be* a Wuu Gappew. "...It explains some things." Only then, something else dawned on him. "But how did you know...?"

"I know all about your reasons for coming here," Bishop Sabracore informed him, his voice affectingly aloof. "And I know all about *you*, Mart Allard. Or, should I say... *Art Mallard*?"

Art gasped. His worst fear was realized all at once. The Cultists weren't just suspicious... they were *wise* to him, and it went all the way to the top...

...But it didn't matter. He couldn't *let* it matter. At any rate, he certainly wasn't about to be backed into a premature confession. He had to consider who he was talking to – a pack of folks all bent out of shape over thumbs. People like that were supposed to be gullible. More than that, he now had every reason to suspect their leader was actually *the most* gullible of them all. Maybe he could still get out of this thing with a bit of clever, subtle trickery. "Art Mallard?!" he asked, taking up an indignant front. "I don't have a clue what you're talking about! I never heard of anyone with a far-out name like that."

A tense silence filled the room with crushing judgment. "I don't care for lies, Mallard." He snapped his tentacle, which sent Therodrux on a beeline for the door. "But then, what else could I expect from you? A charlatan. A man who would feign deep convictions, only to betray the ones who trusted him. An informant... a willing collaborator... a liar in the service of liars. Surely, the worst kind of fraud." He gestured back to the doorway. "But why should you waste your falsehoods on me? Here's one more accustomed to them..."

Therodrux returned with Teresa in tow. It sparked a sudden horror and rage in Art to see them drag her into this... a sweet, innocent young lady, whose only guilt was the misfortune of getting mixed up with the wrong crowd. But after a quick study of her face, he didn't find obvious fright at the Overseer's corralling. Her gaze sank when it met Art's, and he read shame in her features. And suddenly he knew she was guilty of something else. She wasn't being brought around as some sort of leverage... like they might hurt her if he didn't cooperate. No. They were merely showing him the one who'd ratted him out...

"You knew?" he asked her softly.

She nodded with her face down. "I'm sorry."

It was an apology that cut deep. "I'm sorry, too."

"A betrayal for a betrayal," Sabracore doted, joining one pair of tentacles. "That's only fair turnabout, wouldn't you say, Mallard?"

"I guess."

"Good," Sabracore replied, a hint of aggression hemming into the soundscape as he began slowly closing the distance between himself and Art. "Then I think we should proceed in the interest of continued equity. I've already given you what you came here for. Now, supposing you return the favor?"

Art tried to back up, forgetting the recliner behind him. He tumbled backward into it, suddenly seated again. His clumsy display of apprehension was as startling as it was humiliating. He tried to make up for it... tried to look stern, talk tough...

"Never! You'll never get a confession out of me! They're all fingers... *all of them*! They're all grippy things on your hand that grow nails! No one in their right mind gives a *hoot* about any missing phalange!"

"Such *defiance*," Sabracore mocked, now hovering dangerously close to Art. "I've heard it all before. Many are the ones who came here before you, singing the same song. But don't worry. They all left marching to a new tune. They all embraced the truth with open arms, in the end. It just takes... a little *time*..." He flashed with an amused recognition. "Speaking of which... that's a nice timepiece you have there." He pointed to the watch still in Art's hand. "May I see it?"

Art just stared up at the Bishop with a stupefied expression. The request was so banal... so detached from the overall trajectory of forced indoctrination by means of torture. What did he care about the silly watch? But on the other hand, what could Art do, if not indulge his curiosity? What else did he have to forestall the pain that was to come?

Eventually, he extended the watch to Sabracore without a word, hopeless to guess his true peril. Sabracore took it up by the chain, letting it dangle in the air... gently waving. Back... and forth...

Back... and forth...

"Beautiful craftsmanship, isn't it? So intricate. So shiny."

"Yup," Art agreed, admiring his own watch as it swung through the air in front of him... seeing it with a fresh, compelling focus... marveling at the way the light shimmered along the contours. "It cost me a bundle."

"I'm sure," Sabracore agreed. "And what a strange coincidence."

Art watched the time tick away, while an unaccountable calm began to wash over him. "Coincidence?" he asked distantly.

"Yes," Sabracore replied, reaching into the folds of one of his coats. "Wouldn't you know, I have one here that's almost just like it?"

And all at once, there were *two* beautiful watches swinging in the air around Art's head. He lazily looked back and forth from one to the other, the recliner beneath him now comfy as a cloud. As he studied them, he glacially reached a conclusion. "I think mine's still a little fancier," he said.

"I suppose you're right." Art was only vaguely aware that another tentacle reached for another pocket. "You seem to know your watches well, Mallard. How would you rate this one?"

Art blinked heavy while he considered the third watch. "Easily the drabbest one yet," he answered, almost with an easy chuckle. Suddenly, through all the cool informality of this impromptu little timepiece-viewing, Art blinked harder, a nameless suspicion trying to rouse itself somewhere in the far back of his mind. He sat up straighter... "Say, what gives? When does the torture start? I'm never going to give in! Never, never!"

"Don't get ahead of yourself, now," Sabracore said, pushing Art back down into the seat. "You should really see the *rest* of my collection..."

In practiced action, Sabracore drew and literally surrounded Art's field of vision with pocket watches – one in each of his seven coiled tentacles. Art fully meant to protest further against this untoward behavior that so confounded him. He may have even strung together a syllable or two. But after just a few moments of immersion in this veritable chandelier of swinging and ticking, he seemed to lose all track of everything – where he was, what he was doing, his own thoughts... even time itself... the very thing that was so readily available to be told. And the more he tried to take hold of himself, the sleepier he seemed to get...

Yes... that was it... he was getting sleepy. Very, *very* sleepy...

Chapter 6

Horus was coming off another terrible night. The lodgings below deck were very dark and distractingly musky... and somehow managed to be even less comfortable than sitting up while doubled over a mahogany desk. Mostly living out of a train, Horus was used to sleeping through locomotion... but even this failed to mitigate the exceedingly random yawing and pitching of the big boat. Naturally, the little rest he did get was plagued by visions of *the chair*. Without so much as benefit of his favored breakfast, Horus made the morning climb out of that creaking, miserable pit of despair only by sheer force of will...

Fortunately, throwing open the hatch was tantamount to flipping a very large internal switch. Within moments above deck, Horus began to revive. The day was bright, the surf was peaceful now, and each breath was fresher than the last. Even the noisy bustle of the crew delighted him in an odd way... just getting a glimpse of another walk of life. There were oh-so-many iterations of menial labor in the world, and each one of them had its own special flavor. Watching the sailors clean and tend the ship, it was hard not to envy the mindless simplicity of their travail. There was maybe not much glory in it... but on the other hand, he reckoned there were fewer crushing setbacks. He took his time among them, musing as he ambled toward the loft over the cabin at the rear of the cargo ship, where passengers were allowed to convene...

En route, a casual scan of the horizon lengthened some unwanted shadows in his mind. Mixed in with the convoy, Horus spied a handful of military escort frigates. Lest he forget, their country was at war with Despotopia. Not that the thought of being waylaid by the sudden appearance of a mighty Despotopian armada concerned him in the least, of course – such an idea was more of a tasteless joke than anything. He had no anxiety about the war itself. It just tended to remind him of that vacant piece of furniture again... the one that should've been filled by an aging soldier in the case he'd just lost. A man who – according to all Horus, Deborah, and Art could dig up on him – had narrowly survived a couple close shaves in a past Despotopian campaign, and who had very nearly been assigned to a march on Mantid lands, where fate was always a forgone conclusion. With so many near-death experiences to look back on, and being no stranger to the traumas of war, when word came he was shipping out for Despotopia a second time, the man must've convinced himself his number was up. And, thus convinced, it seemed he'd found a way to make it true. He'd gone overboard in transit – about as sure an end as they come. Even with regular hunting of the terrors in the depths to keep shipping lanes open, the odds against a man overboard in the Farjean Sea were astronomical. Never mind that he had nowhere left to swim for...

You're drawing conclusions again, Horus, he told himself.

He looked past the frigates, took a few more deep, refreshing sniffs of ocean water, and kept moving...

But he didn't make it very far before something else demanded his attention. Two sea-hands were struggling under the weight of a barrel astride the ship's gunwale. One was spindly with a greasy bowl cut; the other was short, gruff-looking, and bald on top with long, blanched tufts clinging desperately around the perimeter of his head. Horus couldn't know their right names at first glance, of course, but in an odd way it seemed impossible that they shouldn't be called something very much like "Lintel" and "Spaghetti". He watched them labor only briefly before deciding to involve himself.

"Looks like you boys could use a hand," he called to the sailors. "If you keep trying to roll that barrel up the gunwale like that, it's liable to end up in the drink."

"Aye," *Lintel* grunted through clenched teeth. "That's actually what we're going for, Sir."

Horus looked on perplexed. "You *want* to throw it overboard?"

"That's our charge, at present," the man *Spaghetti* strained to say.

Horus shrugged, finding the whole thing very strange but having nothing else to do but take their word. He walked over and reached under the barrel. With the strength of his large body added to the effort, the load went tumbling into the water below and promptly disappeared in a nifty splash. The two sailing men sighed their relief.

"Much obliged, Sir, much obliged," Lintel said. "It's a rare thing, getting help from a passenger. What will you be peddling, then, I wonder? If you've anything affordable, I might just have to buy one – for a keepsake, as much as a show of my gratitude."

Horus chuckled. "I'm not actually a merchant... I just happen to be headed your way. I'm a lawyer."

"Is that so?" Spaghetti asked, starting to look reserved. "Not a *defense* lawyer, I hope?"

"Yes, I'm afraid so."

Lintel just shrugged it off. "Ah well... everyone has their faults. Thank you just the same."

"My pleasure," Horus said, brushing his pleated pants, noting for the first time a line of rope that was unspooling itself over the railing... evidently tied up to the barrel. This served to deepen the mystery. "Not that it's any of my business, but I do wonder if you might explain why we just...?"

"...Pardon the interruption, Mr. Lawyer," Spaghetti interrupted, "but we're running out of line. Duty calls."

"Oh goodness, yes," Lintel said, hunching down and grabbing the end of the rope. "Here goes," he warned, just as the rope was about to draw taught. He gave it a yank, ripping it loose, and both men engaged their entire faces in a dramatic squinting action...

If their behavior alone was not sufficiently perplexing, notable surprise was added to the mix when, half a moment later, a huge explosion threw a towering splash up over the side of the boat and drenched them all. The rolling torrent seemed to last for ages before finally washing away. Horus stood there dripping for some time, more or less shell-shocked, surrounded by dead and dying fish...

"I guess we should really start using longer rope," Lintel commented at length. "Oh well! Back to the mop buckets..."

"We just tossed an explosive overboard?" Horus managed to ask.

"Aye, Sir – a depth charge, if the term means anything to you."

"Not really," Horus admitted. "Was this some sort of war exercise?"

They laughed while they busied themselves with their mops. "Not hardly," Spaghetti answered. "That's for the frigates to worry about. We use depth charges to ward off sea monsters, is all."

"I see," Horus replied, unsure. "What a relief that we have such potent defenses at our disposal. Although, I confess, I hadn't noticed we were under any sort of attack from a sea monster."

The sailors exchanged another amused look. "I think you underestimate our cleverness, Sir. There weren't never no sea monsters at all!"

Horus pursed his jowls, vainly searching their expressions for answers. "Well, you've certainly outsmarted me. Why drop the bomb if there was no monster to drop it on?"

"Purely preventative," Spaghetti explained. "We figure, the monsters see the explosion from far off, and they decide to stay away before they even have a chance to get curious." He pointed to his head. "It's all basic psychiatry."

"I suppose it was my good fortune to be here for you to explain all this," Horus went on. "I can't imagine what the other passengers are thinking right now. You might consider warning them next time."

Spaghetti shrugged. "It's all standard procedure. Who thinks to warn about that?"

"The defense lawyer has his point, though," Lintel argued. "It's wartime. Folks might get the wrong idea when they see bombs going off."

"War, war, war!" Spaghetti mocked, flailing his mop. "We certainly have done our share of talking *around* it, these last few weeks. What is it on for, anyway, I'd like to know!? What business do we have tangling with Despotopia this time? I haven't had that to my satisfaction."

Lintel turned his nose up at the question. "The High Constable claimed there was just cause."

"That's *not* what he said," Spaghetti insisted. "You've got it all mixed up."

"But he *was* asked in public conference. Pray tell what you heard, then?"

"Well he didn't precisely say anything about a *just cause.* Yes, they asked him why we were going to war, alright... to which he shrugged and said, 'just 'cause'."

"I suppose you got that from your sister."

Spaghetti stuck his jaw out. "I did. She *is* in the press, you know."

"Oh, I know. You've told me a hundred times. Only a mop-head like you would be proud of something like that."

Sensing no further opportunity to learn anything of import, Horus began to step away. "If you'll excuse me, gentlemen, perhaps I'd better be going. I believe I may convey the thanks of all aboard for a thoroughly stimulating morning."

"Couldn't have done it without you, Mr. Lawyer!" Lintel called back, drawn smiling out of his grumbling match with Spaghetti for only a moment before the two were at it again.

Just a quick flight of stairs later and Horus was already in his next social predicament. All the eyes of the passengers were on him, begging some explanation for the commotion, and not much bothering whether they could reasonably expect he had an answer. Fortunately for them, he did anyway...

"No cause for alarm!" he declared, outstretched arms still dripping. "The crew assures me it was only a routine explosion."

The vendors and craftsmen readily accepted this news and went immediately back to milling about. Horus wasn't sure he could've been so easily assuaged in their place, but certainly didn't mind not having to recount the whole dubious episode. He began milling himself, in search of Deborah...

"Nice speech, Boss," she told him as he found her in a lounge chair by the gunwale. "Though if I really stop to think about it, I'm not sure what constitutes a *routine explosion*."

He took the lounge chair adjoining hers. "Apparently, dropping very real bombs on imaginary sea monsters."

"Ah... that's the best kind of sea monsters." She looked skeptically at him over a pair of classy sunglasses. "Looks like you had a front-row seat."

"More than that... I was an accessory."

She grinned sarcastically. "I guess this is what happens when I leave you unsupervised for too long."

"That's exactly right," he nodded. "Best not let it happen again." His expression slowly became more serious as he conspicuously studied the huge book in Deborah's hands. "What's your reading pleasure for the day?"

She turned the binding toward him, so that he could plainly read '*Vilkerracht*'... the formative text for international law. "It's my own copy. But if you forgot yours at home – or if you lost it in the bombing – you're welcome to it. I can always find something else."

"Thank you anyway. I'm sure there will be plenty of time for *Vilkerracht* later."

She furrowed a brow at him. "What *have* you been studying so far? Case files?"

"As a matter of fact, yes."

"Well that's interesting."

"Oh?" he chuckled. "Pray tell why."

"I'm just curious what international incident you could be looking at that would have any bearing on this one. There isn't a long history of Queen custody battles, you know." She was quite right. Without fail – since the beginning of the world – there had been seven Meduseldan Queens... one for each Dominion. For the latest Queens of the Berlie Beirel Dominion – Irisa and Asiri – to have poofed into existence simultaneously at the end of their predecessor's life had therefore caused a bit of a stir. The question of heirship had consumed their lives (and that of their drones) from the first – absolutely paramount as it was ultimately unanswerable...

But he shook his head. "It's not an international case I'm studying," he explained, reaching for his inside pocket. "The thought occurred: I'll be facing Berlie Beirel attorneys in Roemnar... perhaps I ought to start with a cursory look at Berlie Beirel law."

Deborah nodded. "Studying your opponents... that's smart."

Finally, Horus reached his files, frowning as he drew them out soggy. Deborah managed not to laugh at his expense. "You'll have to give me your take on Berlie Beirel law when you're done," she tried instead. "Jelly-culture is a bit esoteric; I can scarcely imagine what their courts are like."

"Rather simplistic, if I may say so," Horus volunteered. "As you might expect, they have an impressively low incidence of crime in their nations... and not much appreciation for the severity of crimes, either."

"They tend to live uncomplicated lives," she agreed.

"Yes... and their argumentation in matters of due process is equally uncomplicated. Primitive, almost."

"How so?"

Horus had to avert his look as he searched for a delicate way of explaining their methods. "Apparently, the final verdict of most cases comes down to two main factors: the relative volume and persistence of one attorney versus the other."

Deborah winced. "You mean whoever shouts loudest and longest wins the case?"

Horus only nodded.

Deborah huffed. "You're putting me on."

Carefully, he opened his soggy transcript. "Allow me to read an excerpt from '*Berlie-Beireldom vs. Maplewarlof*'." He scanned and quickly found the desired passages. "Prosecution: It is my contention that your client is most certainly guilty. Defense: No, he is innocent. Prosecution: No, he is guilty. Defense: No, he is innocent! Prosecution: No, he is guilty!!" After a moment of silence, he set the transcript down.

"...And it just goes on and on like that?" she asked.

"There are seventeen more pages of the same fare, with only the development of steadily-growing chains of exclamation marks."

She shrugged with open palms. "Well... I guess it's only to your benefit. If the prosecutors come to the Annex Tribunal expecting to win that way, they'll have another thing coming." She grinned at him. "If anything, this means you can afford to take it easy the next few days."

He shook his head. "It *means* I should be cautious. These are still professional attorneys, Deborah... Meduseldan attorneys at that. With even a little Dronehood training, they could read *Vilkerracht* ten times before I absorb a single chapter. I can't afford to let myself be lulled into a false sense of security. I need to be at my best. Better, if possible. This case is too important for me to fail."

She considered him... seemingly concerned. "Have you talked with your client again yet?"

Horus froze up a bit. For once, her uncanny sense of things didn't strike him so pleasantly. Given their initial meeting, he wasn't in any hurry to confer with Mo again... at least, not until he could secure certain privileges for him. He reasoned a surprising and dramatic show of goodwill would be enough to clear any pretense of misgivings between them. But until then, well... what more did they really need to talk about, anyway?

He frowned. "Not yet. Right now, I really need to focus on my studies... and get some waivers in order. There should be plenty of time to speak with him after we make landfall."

She grinned slightly, and he was relieved to see her accept his reasoning. "Well, at least see if you can't find some time to relax before then. I certainly mean to."

He grinned back. "I hope you're not mistaking this for a vacation... just because we happen to be sitting in chaise lounges, rubbing elbows with high-rolling businessmen."

"You have to admit it's *a little* vacationy. While we're still sailing, anyway." She buried an uncertain look into her copy of *Vilkerracht*. "I'm frankly trying not to even think about what it's going to be like when we reach Heron country."

"Such apprehension is unwarranted in your case, Ms. Boulevard," the voice of Dr. Nokkaeru intruded into their midst. "It is true: We Roemnari are greatly bothered at the general prospect of entertaining visitors. We prefer our own company, if we must have any company at all. But as visitors go, the two of you will not be found so very offensive."

"How reassuring," Deborah replied. She and Horus watched the doctor approach alongside Miloje, who, despite still being confined to chair, was at least wheeling himself around now.

"Good morning, Doctor, Milo," Horus greeted them. "It's nice to see you've managed to venture above-deck."

Miloje gruffly cleared his throat. "Yes, well... it is a bit of a bother, having to be hauled around wherever steps and ladders would tend to be restrictive. But after all, I had little choice in the matter."

"It amounted to yet another medical intervention," Nokkaeru explained. "His countenance in the bowels of the ship had become so dark, even I began to fear the long-term repercussions. Such is the depth of Human frailty that even perfectly mundane despair seems to take a physical toll after a time. The superficial beauty of nature was all I had on-hand to staunch further deterioration."

"Superficial or no, in the end I do admit to feeling rather staunched," Miloje confessed, taking a deep, leisurely breath as he surveyed the horizon. "I have lived and worked by the ocean all my life, but scarcely do I recall ever taking a moment to appreciate its wonder... its *immensity*. I suppose... if my inevitable demise had to be forestalled in this meaningless fashion... at least I can be thankful for such an occasion."

"Well, seeing as we've caught you in... a *good* mood," Horus began uncomfortably, "would it be too much to inquire about... the procedure? You'll forgive my curiosity, I hope. But I don't presume to know anything about 'heart arrhythmia', much less what could be done about it."

"That goes double for me," Deborah backed him up. "We care about you, Stenya. We'd just as soon be in the know."

Miloje looked questioningly over at Dr. Nokkaeru. "Do you wish to tell them, or shall I?"

"By all means, go ahead," the doctor gestured with an open talon. "It would interest me to hear it in your words... to see how truly you grasp the details of your own ailment."

Miloje fairly scowled. "Very well. Let us all see if a roughneck can expound such lofty matters." He turned and leaned forward in his wheelchair, his eyes glistening at Horus as with secret knowledge. "Do you know, Templar, that the beating of the heart is regulated by electrical impulses?"

"I'm sure I didn't know that," Horus admitted.

"I'm not surprised. But I think it can be excused... considering that even most doctors don't know it."

"Most of *your* doctors," Nokkaeru corrected.

"True enough," Miloje begrudged. "But even among the privy ones, it has been a fact of little value. Knowing that the heart is governed by such impulses is one thing, but meaningful application of that knowledge has so far eluded even the best... until quite recently. You see, it's not so much my heart itself that's at fault. People with heart arrythmia will occasionally send faulty electrical signals... get their valves pumping all out of cadence. Only now, there is a surgical doctor in Roemnar who believes he can implant a device that would effectively regulate the signals... keep a ticker like mine ticking in step, as it were."

"That sounds promising," Horus nodded.

"Yes, but there are several caveats," Miloje went on. "It is a procedure very new and unproven... the device, highly technical... and potentially temperamental."

"...And you may be too old and feeble to survive implantation," Nokkaeru added.

Miloje gave her another sour look. "Yes, I was coming to that on my own, thank you."

"Well, never mind. Quite apart from any mention of nodes, atria and ventricles, I would say you rendered a fair explanation for the layman."

The Deputy Constable bowed in his seat. "I accept your high praise with utmost humility."

It seemed that she looked at him askance, even through her mask. "You are a sarcastic one. Between your candor and your poor condition, I do wonder how you'll be received, when we reach my homeland." She turned her gaze on Horus and Deborah. "Not like the two of you. Counselor Templar especially, I expect will be quite welcome among the people."

Deborah smiled at him sarcastically. "How do you like that? Sounds like you're finally going somewhere you can be popular, Horus."

"Ah, but he will not be the only one," Nokkaeru continued, in an all-too foreboding tone. "Even in Roemnar, the secretarial fame of Deborah Boulevard is renowned."

Before Horus could goad her back, another voice jumped unbidden into the conversation. "*Deborah Boulevard*?" an awed passer-by marveled, instantly chilling the blood of all who heard him. "***The*** Deborah Boulevard? Here?! Within hand-shaking distance?!"

Practically stunned for a moment, Horus finally got a good fix on where the voice was coming from: a man in a tropical shirt, sporting big, obnoxious sunglasses that surely hadn't left his nose since the beginning of his career...

if, in fact, he hadn't simply been born wearing them. Without so much as a conscious thought, Horus discerned that this was a salesman... worse yet, a *salesman's* salesman. And so, like all conscious life, he had to rally and conquer a powerful flight reflex as he sat there, helplessly watching the man reach out and shake his secretary's hand...

"Charmed I'm sure, Mr...?" Deborah forced out breathlessly through her strained smile.

"Snozzwell. Nostradamus Snozzwell, at your service," he offered graciously, though somehow it felt he said precisely the opposite. "What an unexpected pleasure it is to finally meet you," he went on, still shaking her hand. "And who, may I ask, are these adorable little people with you?" He fixed his shaded glance on Horus. "Why, this *must* be your boss... Hogarth Templeton!"

"Horus... to my friends," Horus said, reluctantly accepting the man's hand, if only to relieve poor Deborah.

"Right, right," Snozzwell nodded disinterestedly. "So then, which one of these is your client?" he asked, turning to Nokkaeru and Miloje. "Or is it one of those twofer deals?" He snapped. "And I thought they told me you were going to represent a jellyfish..."

"I..." Horus began, clearing his throat. "That is, I *am* going to be representing a Meduseldan in an upcoming case." His face contorted with an uneasy confusion. "Forgive my impertinence, Sir, but what would *you* have heard about it?"

"Oh, probably all of it, though by now I've forgotten most of the specifics," Snozzwell waved dismissively. "Nothing personal, Harry. I just remember catching wind of a case for the Annex Tribunal, and having my secretary write up a letter to the Chairman of the Trade Office, to see if he could call in some favors and get you assigned to it. Don't you see? It's perfect! This way, we're all headed in the same direction!"

Horus found he couldn't absorb the relevant data fast enough. He *had* been put on Mo's case by arrangement of the Chairman of the Trade Office... Blackforest revealed as much before their departure. That in itself had been curious, to say the least. Now – apparently – it was all revealed to be part of some 'perfect' masterplan devised by a strange salesman he'd never met before...

"You... you arranged all this?" he stammered at length. "But I must be mistaking you somehow. You said only moments ago what an unexpected pleasure this meeting is..."

"Did I say unexpected?" Snozzwell chuckled. "I'm sure I meant unexpected for you. Yes, of course I arranged it! After all, who wouldn't jump through a few flaming hoops for the chance to work with *the* Deborah Boulevard?!"

"Pardon me, Mr. Snozzwell," she interjected. "I'm afraid *the* Deborah Boulevard is also a little confused. I'm Mr. Templar's legal secretary... and you're... clearly some kind of salesman. In what possible way do you propose to work with me?"

"Well, I've got ears, don't I?" Snozzwell argued.

Deborah blanched. "Yes... I think so."

"I do... I *definitely* do. And I heard it same as you... straight from the birdie's mouth." He gestured at a thoroughly put-out looking Dr. Nokkaeru. "You're bigtime, Debby... even in Heron country, you've got *star power*!" he exalted, pumping his fist. "And that's just what The Brand needs to take it to the next level! You, Debby! We need *you*!"

Deborah shook her head, utterly beside herself. "I... I don't understand."

"We call it 'celebrity endorsement' in the bizz," he explained, before turning away, looking a bit sheepish. "I, eh, don't mean to brag, but... I'm a bit of a somebody, myself. That is, I'm the Senior Director of Marketing for Jast-Madiir's fastest-growing corporation, two years running! I don't suppose you know who that is?"

She made what seemed an earnest effort to come up with a guess... but was perhaps still too bewildered by it all to truly deal with a question. She traced little circles in the air with her nose as she tried to think. Finally, he leapt into the sonic void for her...

"Kloggem Mills! Owner, proprietor, and distributor of none other than the one... the *only*... Tasty Chunks Cereal!"

Silence ensued again as they all worked to contain their amazement.

"That... that's monumental," Deborah ventured at last. "And... you want... *me*... to endorse your cereal?"

"*Want* isn't a strong enough word, Debby," Snozzwell said, taking a knee in the midst of his theatrics. "It's just like I said... I *need* you! The Brand needs you! Think of it! We've already cornered the market in Jast-Madiir... we're just one good trade show away from something so much more. If we can sell in Roemnar, we can sell anywhere! We'll go international! We'll go worldwide! We'll be unstoppable. And all we need to do it is the right face. *Your* face." He held his arms outstretched to her. "Debby... I'm going to make *you* the face of Tasty Chunks!"

She couldn't help her muzzle curling up in pure disgust. It was like a nightmare, except much worse. Not with a fever of a hundred and four could she have dreamt-up something so bizarre and unwanted. Only this was no dream... it was *real*. She was horrified. Even Nokkaeru and Miloje – poor, innocent bystanders that they were – looked horrified. But all their collective horror – ran through one or more exponential computations – could not compete with what Horus felt in that moment, listening-in while the details of his world's obliteration were casually discussed...

He couldn't stand idly by...

"Now look here, Mr. Snozzwell..." he began, slowly realizing that he was standing over the little salesman like a storm-cloud about to burst. He retracted an accusatory finger, composing himself. "Your business proposition is certainly... well... *interesting*. But I'm afraid Ms. Boulevard is not at present liberty to entertain commercial ventures of any sort. She *is* retained as my personal legal secretary, and we are, as you know, currently engaged in a case of international import. Moreover, it is a case – I am assured – of personal interest to the Czarina."

Snozzwell got up, shook his head. Then he reached into his tropical shirt. "Not as much interest as her star corporation making a big splash at this year's trade show." He produced a document. "I have a writ, enlisting Deborah Boulevard to the service of Kloggem Mills for the duration of the exhibition."

Horus snatched the writ, scanning it with furious, desperate eyes. "This does appear very official," he admitted reluctantly.

"Endorsed at the highest level," Snozzwell crowed. "Harry, baby... your secretary's an icon... why fight it? There's no harm! She can still help with your legal junk in between public appearances!" He held up a hand with fingers crossed. "I promise, it'll all be totally non-invasive. You won't even notice she's gone. And after the show, things go back to normal anyway!"

Horus pointed frenetically at a line in the writ. "This says you have seven months to pick up an option to contract her permanently!"

Snozzwell shrugged defensively. "Okay, so I have an option... big deal, right? An option's only an option... nothing to get all excited about. Relax, Harry! Your secretary's in good hands. For now. Maybe forever later... but only for now... for now."

Horus nearly took another big step forward, ready to rejoin the argument with renewed gusto, assuming he didn't casually flatten the man in his mere advance. But just then, he felt Deborah hold him back...

"It's alright, Horus," she said. "Everything will be alright."

He looked back at her. As far as he knew, she had never lied to him before, as it was clear she was doing now. But her false assurances carried with them a heavy truth: There was nothing he could do. There was nothing *either* of them could do...

"See? What'd I tell ya?" Snozzwell persisted, effectively rubbing dirt in the wound. "It's all good!" It was all Horus could do to let the words pass him by. "Now, Debby, say you and I go for a little walk around the ship. I've got a full itinerary planned, and you gotta be brought up to speed on all of it!"

She shook her head. "But we were just brushing-up on international law. You said your commercial enterprise wouldn't get in the way of my legal duties..."

"It won't, Debby... it *won't*!" he reassured in urgent, hushed tones, patting her on the shoulder. "Only, maybe it will, just a *liiiiiittle* bit." He made that childish pinching gesture. Then, he led her away, launching into a spirited exposition of all the public endorsements she was going to give, quite likely from the beginning of the trade show until the very end of forever. She looked back at Horus only once, heroically trying to assuage his trauma with a sympathetic half-grin, half-frown. He did his best to return the look...

"Well, that proved quite refreshing, in the end," Dr. Nokkaeru framed it. "This trip promises to be far more restorative than I'd hoped."

Chapter 7

Art awoke with a screaming headache, feeling about as rested as the last time he went a full week without sleep. Once he willed himself to sit up – a major effort in and of itself – he racked his hazy brain while he cradled his throbbing head. Where had he left off? He forced his eyes open, watching the sparkles slowly recede until all that was left was a dark, empty room. A bit of torchlight reached through a small, barred window on the door, so that he could just make out the walls and the concrete slab he'd been sleeping on. But there was nothing else – no cues to help him remember anything...

But of course, it was the Cultists. Yes, they'd found out about him somehow. Therodrux had chloroformed him and... and... then he'd been thrown in here? *No.* No... the rest of it had happened, too: the long wait for the Bishop... the meeting... the betrayal... and... and *more*. Quite an awful *lot* more, it seemed like. But *what*? Why couldn't he remember? What was stopping him?

He did his best to replay his memory of Bishop Sabracore. It was all there – the shock, the fear – up to the very moment he announced he would never give in. Never, never! And then... *nothing*. Nothing but a dubious recollection of being shown some pocket watches...

...That, and a strange, nagging new sense that maybe – just *maybe* – there was a side to this thing that begged further consideration. Was there at least a *chance* that the thumb wasn't all he'd believed it to be his whole life? He had to admit it was possible. Perhaps he'd been too hasty, writing that possibility off from the start...

Art groaned, falling back on his slab. What was he *thinking*? These were the hooligans who'd kidnapped him, imprisoned him, and in some fashion or other, given him a doozy of a headache. They were evil, and their crazy notions had to be equally evil. Now was not the time to take a softer view. The game was afoot, and he was going to have to stick to his guns if he wanted to get out alive, and still in possession of his mental faculties. Particularly if he wanted to get out by *Friday*...

What he needed most urgently of all was a parley with his captors...

This was soon to be. Moments after devising a brilliant plan of escape, he heard the shuffle of footsteps a room or two away... smelled the aroma of something delicious. Or anyway, something that *had* been delicious before some misguided oaf went and cooked it...

He sat back up. The steps grew loud and close, and the smell sensational... almost overwhelming. A pair of mean eyes darkened his little window and he heard the latch on the door slide loose... a sharp clatter like a bolt driven straight into his eardrums. He tried to appear stern and gruff despite what must've been the worst headache and nausea of his life, staring up into the glare of Therodrux's two goons as they let themselves into his cell. They stood silently... disapprovingly... until the one carrying a plate finally handed it off to him...

For his part, Art received the plate. He looked slowly down at it... then defiantly back up. "*Never,*" he said.

Goon #1 folded his arms. "You're not going to eat that?"

"Oh, I'll eat it, alright," Art qualified. "But I'll never go in for your messed-up beliefs. Never, never, never!" His ears folded at the painful intensity of his own protest.

Goon #1 shrugged. "Whatever you say." And they turned to leave.

About the time the door closed, Art fought past the gag reflex to put the next phase of his plan into action. He began noisily, aggressively eating the food they'd brought him, sure to scarf so exaggeratedly that even Human ears wouldn't fail to hear him. After the first few bites, he surprised himself how easy it was... the nausea was gone, and even cooked, the food went down effortlessly. He scarfed long after he'd made his point, shoveling mouthfuls. It was like he hadn't eaten for days...

He went on to feel much better after the binge. He was cozy... relaxed. He was downright drowsy. He found himself fending off the urge to go right back to sleep for quite a long time, as if he needed to reassure himself that his food hadn't been spiked. But after fighting for what seemed long enough to be sure he wasn't under some foreign influence, there was nothing left to keep him awake any longer. He may well have dozed-off the moment his head came back to rest on the slab...

* * *

The next time he woke up, things were different. Yes, it was the same dark room, where no daylight seemed to reach. He was still a groggy prisoner, riddled with the aches and pains of hours spent resting on bare concrete. But such discomfort was superficial now. Sitting and stretching, he really felt rather refreshed. Judging by his general pep and the sheer volume of eye-crust alone, he was quite sure he'd enjoyed a full night's restorative sleep. It certainly begged the question of why he'd awoken so exhausted before, but for the moment he was unconcerned. Today – whatever day it was – was surely the day after he'd last interacted with his captors. Crucial time had passed... time they obviously expected to weaken his resolve... to make him *crack*. Yes, it was beyond simple... they would hold him here until the stir of the slammer made him pliable... willing to believe anything if only to be turned loose. And as far as they knew, they were already getting to him. Behind closed doors, he'd been desperate for the scraps they'd sent his way. Next to that, a few brave words of resistance meant very little, except that he might be trying to convince *himself* he still had the nerve to fight, as much as anyone...

But this was where that nerve would fail him, he'd decided. '*Never, never, never*!' was going to come today...

First, he needed to rough himself up a bit. He ripped the buttons clear of his cuffs, disheveled his collar, tore the elbows of his sleeves, and thanked his lucky stars his alias had obliged him to wear his cheapest shirt. Then he threw himself at the door...

"Hey, are you listening out there?!" Art called, sticking his snout through the little bars as he gripped them. "I've changed my mind! I've seen the light! The thumb is a digit! You hear me!? A **digit**! I'll write it on the blackboard a thousand times! I'll sing it from the rooftops! I'll chase down the first Inquisitor I come across and argue it out until I'm blue in the face! I'll do whatever you want, only don't leave me in here! I can't take it! I just can't take it anymore!"

Thankfully, this attracted some attention. As he watched the hall – an uncannily familiar hall, he noted – a new pair of goons appeared mere moments after his outburst. They found him still clinging to the bars of his window in apparent white-knuckle fashion... though of course his knuckles were much too furry to be positive.

"Step back," Goon #3 instructed. Since the first pair had been named Goon #1 and Goon #2, it only made sense that these two should be named Goon #3 and Goon #4. Art obliged Goon #3 with conspicuous reluctance, trying to appear as raving mad with cabin fever as he could.

Sure enough, they unbolted the door. They came in and stood as a unified front, searching Art with sour, doubting faces. "Are you *really* convinced?" the Goon questioned. "*All the way*... deep into the bedrock of your being? Does it permeate each fiber and sinew? Do you have the conviction to hold this truth self-evident – come what may – from now until the very end of your days?"

Art nodded. "Yup."

The goons gauged each other's reaction. Then, they also nodded. "Follow us. And don't get any bright ideas."

Art had to stifle a smile. He'd already *had* his bright idea, and they'd walked right into it...

Just a few steps beyond the cell, and some pieces of the puzzle were fitting together. In a vague sense, he now knew where he was. His first look through the window of his cell had triggered recognition in the back of his mind, but stepping out had been almost dream-like, in the way it apparently transported him through time and space to a familiar place. Of course, this was not the *same* place... just one built to similar specifications. It was a series of office rooms and other functional spaces built under an old, abandoned warehouse. Newer, larger warehouses built closer to the coast had led to the rapid dereliction of several old buildings just like this, each left to be slowly reclaimed by nature, as the school buildings had been. This particular warehouse had apparently endured the misfortune of being secretly seized and repurposed by the Digit Cults. Art had considerable knowledge of the fate of at least one other warehouse... but there was no use thinking about that now. Rather, he simply allowed himself a moment to enjoy the fact that he'd figured something out, just like an ingenious investigator with untold powers of observation *should* do, every once in a while...

More than that, he accurately predicted their trajectory. They led him to the far end of the hall... no doubt, to the biggest room at the very end. He had every confidence that this was the space they'd converted to the Bishop's Sanctum...

This thought gave him pause. The idea of coming into Sabracore's presence again, much less trying to pull one over on him and swear off the thumb as a finger forever, filled him with even more dread than he'd feared. But he'd made it *this* far, and this was his only gambit. He couldn't risk fighting his way out. Above all, he *needed* to get out alive, and report what he'd learned back to the SAPD, so all this madness could finally be brought to an end...

Mustering grit and stepping into the Sanctum, a quick study of the room revealed striking new data, allowing Art to reconstruct a definite timeline of his captivity. Calling once more on those untold powers of observation, he deftly noted the subtle way that the Cultists had marked off every day on the calendar up to Wednesday. He blanched... that meant it was already Thursday! They'd brought him in on Sunday night... where had all those days *gone*?! It was deeply unsettling to have no idea where so much time had vanished to... not to mention how close he'd come to missing *Friday*...

Fortunately, his investigator eyes revealed good news, as well. There was no sign of Sabracore, much to his great relief. It was only Overseer Therodrux... an unsettling man in his own right, but orders of magnitude better than having to confront the true master of the Cults again. It did strike him a little strange that Therodrux could accept his pledge now, but perhaps having already plied his devices, Sabracore had since moved on, confident Art's captivity would simply run its natural course. Whatever the case, it seemed the Bishop was out...

"Well, here we are again, Mr. Allard," Therodrux said ominously, grinning as he swiveled in his seat to meet him.

"Hey, there... Supreme Elevated Grand Master Overseer," Art responded timidly, hoping to convey regret. "Listen... I know I said some things... thought some things... *did* some things... that were pretty dumb. I'm ashamed of doubting the obvious facts. I'm ashamed of betraying your trust." He forced a sigh. "I wish you wouldn't call me 'Mr. Allard'. It hurts to be reminded of my deception. You know and I know: I'm not Mart Allard. I never was."

Therodrux hesitated. "No," he said at length. "But you *could* be. Why not embrace the name of your true self... the one who rejects the lies of the world? Are you ready to become that man? Are you ready to set aside Art Mallard forever, and take up the mantle of Mart Allard?"

Art blinked. "Well, that's still not really my name... but sure! Why not?"

Therodrux smiled even broader. "A discerning answer. Perhaps you *are* ready..."

He stood, squared with Art, and raised his hand, thumb extended straight down. Art's heart leapt. He'd come again to the worst part of his assignment. Whether it was in the ear of Therodrux, Sabracore, or anyone at all, just about the last thing he wanted to do was actually swear to something he didn't truly believe. But he knew he would never leave this place otherwise, and he'd much rather do it while he was still in his right mind. So he raised his hand, gave the thumbs-down, crossed the fingers of his other hand behind his back, and resolved to get over it later...

That very moment, his sharp ears detected a disruption: shouting and clatter outside... by the foot of the stairway, he guessed. Therodrux immediately sensed something amiss, whether it was because he read the surprise on Art's face, or because his own ears weren't half bad, either. He broke away from their little pledge stance, turning an anxious look on one of his goons.

Goon #3 checked the window. The others in the room awaited his assessment breathlessly as the din continued... grew closer. "Looks like trouble, Master Overseer," he said finally.

"Go and deal with it," Therodrux commanded, trying to mask anxiety with impatience. The Goons of Therodrux nodded, dutifully gathered by the door, and leapt out...

Art was rigid, trapped in a mental turnstile of disbelief, fear, and hopeful expectation as the chaos outside escalated. There were more shouts, and louder... and then a *gunshot*. The compounding tension was just too much to process. Moments passed like hours compressed into seconds...

And then, to his final amazement, three police officers burst into the Sanctum...

"Spread out," a sergeant instructed privates Humphrey and Frid, leveling his musket directly at Therodrux. "Check for hidden escape routes."

"Yes, sir," Private Humphrey replied as the two men began a quick examination of the room.

"Heavens to Betsy, I can't believe you're really here!" Art elated as his swooning brain caught up with the situation. "You found me! You actually found me!"

The police sergeant gave him a questioning look. "You're the investigator, aren't you? Mallard?"

"Yes!" Art replied, suddenly realizing he had his hands up, as Therodrux did. He put them down and cleared his throat. "Yes. That's me."

"Good," the sergeant nodded. "We thought we'd lost you for a while there. I hope it's some consolation that you were here to see us bring in the Master Overseer, and wrap up this Cult case for good."

Art blinked. "But the Bishop! Have you got the Bishop?! You can't let *him* get away!"

The officer's eyes darted momentarily to Therodrux, then back to Art. Humphrey and Frid ended their search and fell back into formation behind him, even as he began to lower his gun. "Bishop, you say? Who's this Bishop?"

"He's the secret leader... the one I told Blucille about!" Art explained energetically, almost frantic. "He's the next level over the Overseer! If you don't find him, we're cooked! All this will be for nothing."

The face of the sergeant drew back in a strange way... like he regarded Art with doubt... or even some level of disgust. "Alright, then... describe him. Who should we be looking for?"

"He's Meduseldan... a Wuu Gappew named Sabracore. He wears scary black cloaks and travels with a lot of pocket watches."

The sergeant set his jaw, appearing downright unimpressed. "I see."

Art's puzzler set to work again as he watched the cops simply stand around at ease for long seconds. His eyes shifted furiously between them for answers. Just as he'd given them the lead they'd sorely sought for many months, it seemed all sense of urgency had promptly flown from the room...

"Well, come on now!" he prodded them at length. "Can't you guys see how heavy this is? You need to find him pronto! You need to find Sabracore! He's getting away!"

"But I've never gone, Mallard," the calm but eerily present voice of Sabracore assured him. He floated casually through the doorway in the next moment...

Before he could point and shout, *'There he is; nab him!'* Art saw that the curtain was being pulled back on some sort of grandiose illusion. Though his head was spinning full-speed, he couldn't piece it all together in the moment. He could only watch as Bishop Sabracore coasted to the forefront while the policemen looked on with a sort of prideful amusement, with Goons #3 and 4 returning from the hall, unharmed. The players, it seemed, had all gathered for the final bow. But what was the play?

Finally, in an instant of terrible epiphany, he felt he understood...

"This... this was all a ruse," he began simply enough. "A big stunt to see if I would sell you out, given the chance."

"Oh, very good," Sabracore congratulated him with a single clap. "You've upheld your reputation as an investigator. Tell me... what else have we learned?"

Art looked past him at the policemen. He choked out the words. "Well it... it looks like you've converted some coppers."

Sabracore bobbed as if to nod. "I'm sure it looks that way. But come on now, Mallard, think harder! Anyone can put on a uniform and play pretend. These aren't *real* policemen."

Art shook his head. "But Private Humphrey... Private Frid! I know these men! I've met them before!"

"Have you, now?" Sabracore asked, aglow with derisive amusement. "And when precisely was that? What was the occasion?"

"It was..."

Art's eyes bulged. No answer was forthcoming. He turned his memory banks inside-out, and still came up blank. It wasn't even on the tip of his tongue. Whatever he was searching for had altogether vanished from existence...

"I... I don't know."

"Now don't be modest," Sabracore mocked. "You've already proven your talent for solving capers. I'm confident you can remember... if you just look a little *closer*..."

Art obliged, squinting with exertion as he studied the beat cops again. And suddenly – almost magically – recognition struck like a bolt of lightning. He kept looking on in disbelief. The men had seemingly transformed before his eyes. Their contemptuous, disgustingly pleased faces were the same, but all the data in his head surrounding them changed in an instant. Sabracore was right. They weren't cops at all...

"Gadzooks!" he exclaimed. "It's Goon 1 and Goon 2!" He grabbed his small head, with naught to do for his incredulous brain but try to physically prop it up. "But how did I... they... they were just... but I saw..."

"You saw what I told you to see," the Bishop explained. "There was never any Private Humphrey or Private Frid. Those were identities I suggested to your subconscious mind. I set the conditions for you to recognize them as such... and it was only at my prompting that you see them now as they are."

"You?" Art asked in horror, as more grim theories began to metastasize. "Yes... of course it was you. You and your 'powers of persuasion', no doubt. That must be where all those missing days went. You've been messing with my head! What did you do to me? What've you been doing to my brain?"

"Just a little benevolent rearranging," Sabracore answered with a shrug. "You wouldn't accept the truth on your own. You left me no choice but to program it into you."

"Then what was all this song and dance about?" Art challenged. "What does planting false acquaintances have to do with thumb doctrine?"

"Well, don't forget... I've been at this a long time. I find it helpful to give my subjects a glimpse of what I can do. It helps make them more pliable in the long run. Suggesting memories is one bit of work. Replacing core beliefs, now... that tends to take real persistence." He reached for a pocket, drawing up a gilded little chain, securing the small watch on the end with another tentacle. "Speaking of which, I'd say it's high-time for your next treatment..."

"Forget it," Art defied him, crossing his arms. "The jig is up, Sabracore. You just blew the lid off your own little game. If you think you can dupe me with the pocket-watch trick a second time, you're out of your gourd!"

Art's words quickly shrunk into nothing more than a lingering whiff of embarrassment. Whatever emotion held the room in oppressive stasis, no one was smiling at his expense anymore. One thing felt clear: He was *wrong*. So wrong, it wasn't even funny...

The silent tension burst as Sabracore finally let the watch fall to the end of its chain. Scarcely had it jumped and jangled, and the room was swept away in a fractal vortex of mental framework Art hadn't even remembered being laid...

TICK... TOCK...

The tiny hands on the clockface several yards ahead of him percussed mercilessly – a steady, world-rippling throb, and much too slow...

TICK... TOCK...

No matter how he careened... no matter his sense of weightless vertigo... he could feel his feet still anchored on an invisible floor. And whatever dramatic sensory effects pounced for his attention – however he tried to look away – Sabracore's swinging watch remained fixed before his unblinking eyes...

"You're a simple man at heart, Mallard," Sabracore crisply expounded over the din of his world-clock counting off the ages. "I admit, the simple ones take the most work. But as you can see, we've made more progress than you think."

"No," Art resisted, barely registering his own voice. "I... I don't have to listen to you. None of this is real."

"Reality is truth, and the truth is what I tell you. Consider yourself fortunate you've been chosen to be part of this great undertaking. We have so many lies to roll back... thumbs are only a glorious beginning. Color harmonies... the dwarf planet being passed-off as one of the Other Worlds... the many secret things they don't want us to know about Non-Entities... it must *all* be brought to light. And you... simple Artimus Mallard... you're going to help us. You're going to *want* to help us. You'll be tripping over your own feet to herald our revolution to the far corners of the world. And you'll joyfully spit your last breath at the ignorance you now cling to. So why waste another moment? You'll only live to regret it... especially if you force me to make this unpleasant for you. Why not rather see reason now?"

"I won't," Art chanted emptily, though he forced all his thought into the words. "I won't."

"Oh, you *will*. Soon enough, I'll show you."

Chapter 8

"I'm not satisfied we have the whole picture," Horus said, in a vaguely echoey voice, staring off into the unsearchable brightness outside his car window. "We've been told Private Maloney was the last one to see him – around 8:30. But he wasn't reported missing until promptly at 12 o'clock. Surely three and half hours is too long to go unaccounted-for on a ship. Maloney didn't even remember anything peculiar in his initial statement. I doubt very much our man went directly overboard from there. Someone else must've seen him. Either we don't have the timeline reconstructed right, or someone knows more than he's telling. Whichever it is, we'll get to the bottom of it. We'll subpoena the whole crew if we have to..."

Suddenly, Horus was uncomfortably aware of his own monologuing. The room was oddly quiet. No breathing, no shifting... no scratch of pen on paper...

"...Are you getting all this, Deborah?" he asked, feeling anxiety clench his gut and prickle his extremities...

"Deborah?"

The sound of a knock on the door providentially woke him just before his mind's eye could wander to the ghastly sight of another empty chair. Drawn abruptly back into the waking world from the dreamy one, he neither jumped nor started. He was just too tired for it now... and as things presently stood, neither world was any relief from the other...

Slow to become truly alert, he was conscious of some irony: He was sitting in a chair himself – the only one in his entire little bungalow, rare commodity as such furniture was in Roemnar. He remembered now, sitting with only the intention of removing his shoes. But he'd found the chair comfortable, and himself lethargic. And somewhere in a few minutes' idle staring, he must've simply dozed off...

KNOCK-KNOCK

Ah yes, the door, Horus thought absently. It might've been cause for urgency, if he'd had any real hope that it was Deborah on furlough from her new job in advertising. But his instincts served him better than that... and anyway, he would have recognized the knock. Drawing himself up anyway and straightening his suit, he crossed the wide, dim, circular expanse. On the way, he resolved to open some windows after he'd invited this unexpected caller in, only to remember suddenly that they *were* open. As with everything in Roemnar he'd so far encountered, this temporary abode of his was built into the ground, rather than on it, with only a narrow encircling trench to allow access. There simply wasn't much daylight to be had, down in those tight quarters... whether here or anywhere else in the settlement. As far as he could tell, it seemed the Herons had taken a gently-rolling, idyllic country vista and quite intentionally carved it all up into a dim and dreary, open-pit concrete labyrinth. Perhaps it was only an effect of his own melancholy, but for some odd reason that kind of city planning on their part didn't much surprise him...

As he opened his door, he was reminded why not...

"Greetings, Counselor," Dr. Nokkaeru offered, as she darkened his already dark doorway.

"Good morning," Horus replied, as thoughts of inviting his caller in began to sour. "This is most unexpected, Doctor... what brings you here?"

"I am here to recruit your services for the day," she answered.

His brows scrunched. "My services?" An amusing theory occurred to him. "Are you in some sort of legal trouble?"

"I do not mean your services as an attorney," she clarified, "but rather, as an upright creature with dexterous forelegs. Our mutual acquaintance the Deputy Constable demands to attend the trade show. But he is in no condition to wheel himself around for hours on end, and I flatly refuse to maneuver him with my face."

Horus shook his head. "No doubt. But then... you *do* have wings."

"And also my dignity." She ruffled her wings along her flanks. "Would you have me use these as if they were mean arms? Not in your own anthropomorphic lands, Counselor... and certainly not here."

He scratched his chin and sighed. "Well, I don't wish to disappoint the Deputy Constable... but you do understand, my case is about to begin. I still have many preparations to make."

"Without benefit of your secretary, no less. It is not as if I have forgotten your miseries... far be it from me to do so. But fear not; I have considered your need and arranged for a worthy substitute myself." She turned and craned her head around the bend of the trench. "Jether!" she called. "Come here at once."

Horus watched while a smaller Heron wobbled up to Nokkaeru's side. With his off-color plumage, crown of thin feather quills and awkward, downy complexion – not to mention his stature – it was immediately clear that this was a youngster. Horus had never seen a juvenile Heron before... nor did he have the faintest idea why he was seeing one now...

"Horus Templar, this is my nephew, Jether," Nokkaeru said, by way of introduction. For his part, Horus was too lost in his puzzlement to say anything right off. Young Jether only twisted his head disinterestedly on a coiled neck, until his aunt nudged him...

"Hello, Horus," he said. She nudged him again. "That is, Mr. Templar."

"Nice to meet you, Jether," Horus nodded cordially. But then he turned back to Nokkaeru. "It never occurred to me you might have relatives, Doctor," he admitted before he could catch himself. He cleared his throat. "What an unlikely privilege to meet one in person. But tell me: To what do I owe the pleasure?"

"Well, by stroke of good fortune, it seems this young sister-son of mine has shown tremendous interest in the work of a legal aide."

"I said that like once when I was a five and half weeks old!" Jether whined.

"Hush yourself, child!" Nokkaeru admonished in a hoarse whisper. "Once is enough to be binding. What vocation have you shown interest in since? Answer me that! You must certainly study *something* until you are placed in your permanent trade. An apprenticeship such as this will be good for you."

Horus blanched. "Apprenticeship?" He lacked for more words. "I... but surely you understand I don't have time for... that is... an internship will only mean *more* work for me, not less. I couldn't possibly spare the time to introduce this young man to legal practice."

"Well now, wait just a minute, Mr. Templar," Jether piped-up, suddenly on the defensive. "Like, okay, maybe I want out of this as much as you do... but I don't have to stand here and listen to you talk about me like I don't know what I'm doing. After all, this isn't my first winter."

"It most certainly is," Nokkaeru corrected.

"Okay, *fine*! But you know what I mean! It's not like I'm just some dopey little kid anymore! I digest my own food now, thank you very much... and I already know plenty about dumb legal stuff! Certainly more than enough to be this guy's secretary for a case or two!"

Nokkaeru nodded. "Very good. It's settled, then."

Jether and Horus alternated horrified looks between each other and the doctor. "It most certainly is *not* settled," Horus finally objected. "Much as I... *appreciate*... the offer, I feel it is unnecessary, and ultimately untenable. If

I'm left in peace for a few more days, I should be able to handle this case with only occasional help from my own secretary."

"What occasional help do you mean?" Nokkaeru challenged. "You know as well as I that the man Snozzwell's assurances of shared custody were flagrant falsehoods. I daresay this outing will likely be your only chance to see the Secretary Boulevard for the duration of the trade show... and even after that, you must consider that your odds of reuniting with her are dubious. Now be a good fellow and come along, lest you should fail to fulfill what may well be a friend and colleague's dying wish. And afterwards accept the help of my nephew Jether. I cannot promise you he will not be a thorn in your side, but I *can* promise he will not be a thorn in *mine*... never mind that his parents seem to think they can foist him off on me any time I happen to be stateside. But enough from you both! Onwards! Let us be off!"

Horus surprised himself, obliging her as if at the command of his own mother...

* * *

Though doubts about his future – both immediate and long-term – were at an all-time high, Horus found himself blessed once again by the simple restorative power of being outside. Walking the sunken streets of Roemnar was a far cry from enjoying nature at its most bounteous, of course. The air was still and unscented. The sky was narrow and colorless above him, and all around, he yearned for the sight of anything green, blue, or even brown. So much as a wet spot or a crack with a rogue blade of grass in their stony surroundings might've reassured him. But if there were any such defects, it wasn't his luck to find them. Even the insects – if there were any – feared to speak out of turn here. The Herons not only presided over Roemnar... they *dominated* it, with a powerful indifference that it seemed even nature itself could not rival...

...But on the other hand, at least it was a little brighter out here...

As he wheeled Miloje onward, Horus' relief steadily grew, the closer they got to the big trade show. The foot-traffic on the streets was denser here, and his ears were bombarded with familiar bustling and clatter, so that things began to feel a bit more like home. He smiled openly when he first caught sight of Human merchants... good-old sloppy, noisy, ungainly Humans, each literally calling out for attention to a thrall of birds that seemed to have congregated for the express purpose of ignoring them...

BANG!

Horus' ears and eyes snapped to the source of the explosion, catching sight of a dense smoke-cloud puffing from somewhere in the rear of a strange chattering contraption in the rough shape of a horse. It sputtered and jumped on piston-legs that drummed the pavement with lightning speed and ferocity for several seconds, until a Despotopian man came up and shut the crazy thing off. Horus approached the scene, his sudden start having quickly given way to wonder and curiosity...

"You see, ve vill replace zee standard horse! Zhis innovation vill revolutionize personal transportation! It vill not tire! It can run for hours... on just a few briskets of coal! You can ride it anyvhere you vish!"

"What would make us want to ride it anywhere?" one Heron challenged. "We can fly."

The Herons walked away, leaving a very droopy-looking Despotopian alone with his mechanical beast. Horus just shook his head. Even he had to pity the adorable, incurable fallibility of Despotopians at times...

Just as he turned to move on himself, he found his way unexpectedly blocked. A very distinguished, very elderly Heron stood before him, studying him with milky, sightless eyes. And arrayed about him, there was a considerable entourage of Heron commoners, each considering Horus in like fashion...

"Here is the one whose coming I spoke of..." the Old Heron declared to his followers.

At this, Horus perked up, feeling suddenly to be of some prophetic importance. He knew full-well the strange precognitive powers that some Dire Herons boasted... particularly the ones with bad eyes...

"...Here is the one that something *terrible* will happen to," the Old Heron concluded.

The group of Herons nodded amongst themselves, even offering a few vaguely interested murmurs, before their Old master and the lot of them veered off and continued down the street, leaving Horus in a worse funk than before...

"Did I not say you would be adored here?" Nokkaeru doted on him.

Before Horus could say anything in his huff, Miloje stirred in his seat. "I say, let's have a gander over there!" he exclaimed, pointing and nearly leaping at some booths across the way that had apparently piqued his interest. Horus was glad to comply and move on...

As they approached, wonders met their eyes that seemed more at home in a circus than at a convention for selling wares... bright flashes and errant shadows – men and women juggling fireballs, guiding wild whisps of water through intricate paths in the air... all as if by some sort of magic. Until suddenly, it dawned on Horus... magic was *precisely* what they were using. These were no illusory marvels... they were *real*...

"*Real magic*," he breathed. "I've heard it was out there... but I'd nearly given up on ever seeing it."

"You're likely to see a good deal more of it in the coming years," Miloje boded over his shoulder. "It's becoming commonplace among mercenaries. The Czarina wants it for the military. And she recognizes its commercial implications."

Horus shook his head, even if Miloje couldn't see it. "Surely the Inquisition will never allow it."

"The Inquisition isn't sure what to do, in the absence of Enscharaulgk," Miloje explained. "They'd rather wait and see what he has to say about it before they go and mettle in national policies. You have to admit, it was rather innocently discovered."

"A lot of dangerous things are."

Their discussion trailed off naturally as they came to within point-blank range of the mystical exhibition. Things not quite as flashy as the fireballs and flying waterworks proved even more impressive up close, so that Miloje was struggling to sit high enough to get a good view. They lingered some time by a booth where a man sat between two sorcerers... one using some sort of dark magic to open old wounds on his hand, the other using a pale, bright magic to seal them back up...

"Now, *this* is interesting," Miloje commented... familiar, playful sarcasm creeping into his voice. "Looks like you're verging on obsolescence, Doctor. Any oaf with a little magic could do your job, faster and better. Perhaps I've been looking for my solutions in the wrong place."

Nokkaeru shook her head. "Life Magic is hardly more than cosmetic... used to treat open wounds and surface traumas, in the most remarkable circumstances. It would take an extraordinarily powerful sorcerer to heal anything more serious than the abrasions on display here... power so exclusive, none dare try to attain it. Indeed, unless you could find someone of truly momentous Purpose, your confidence in a magical cure would be sorely misplaced."

"I would expect to hear nothing less from one whose craft has run its course," he goaded her. "Still, you may be right about Life Magic. Even so... an old cop with nothing left to lose can't help keeping his eyes open."

They passed all the magical booths, pausing to appreciate each one... until they came to a final, smaller booth that was sort of pushed back into the corner. Here they found two vendors – by all appearances, a brother and a sister – who just sat a few feet apart, looking bored and glum.

"Hullo there," Miloje called to them. "Pray tell, what magics would you be peddling in?"

They exchanged an unhopeful look before returning to their prospective customers. "I have Positive Magic," the sister answered.

"And I have Negative Magic," the brother continued.

"Really?" Horus chimed. "I would've thought you were both negative."

No one laughed at his joke.

"I think you're going to have to elaborate on that, my friends," Miloje invited them. "I'm afraid I don't quite follow as stated."

They hesitated, as if whatever exotic powers they boasted were no better than an embarrassment to them. But finally, they held up their pointer fingers – each toward the other – and a small bolt of lightning flickered in the open space between them. Horus and Miloje jumped. If not for their extremely practiced apathy, Nokkaeru and Jether might've jumped, too...

"That's how electrical power works," the sister explained. "You need both Positive and Negative."

"Basically one power for the price of two," the brother elaborated further.

"Rather a shame," Horus commented.

But Miloje only stroked his mustache thoughtfully...

"And, two Magics in one person?" he asked at length. "Not possible, I suppose?"

"I can't see how," the brother shrugged.

"It's understood that if you drink two different magic elixirs, one just overwrites the other," the sister went on.

"Which is good, I guess," the brother continued. "Makes it harder to accidentally max-out your Purpose."

"I see," Miloje nodded, though he seemed far off in his thoughts by now.

"I think we have lingered long enough among these parlor tricksters," Nokkaeru stated unabashedly. "Let us continue on to more reputable wares."

* * *

The show stretched on and on, with uncounted booths hailing from all nations in the Archipelago. Even Maenea had brought goods to peddle. The only item Horus noted among their trinkets was a heavy iron press, whose apparent use was to stamp patterns into coins. It was certainly novel, if only because he knew it would be highly illegal back in Jast-Madiir, where defacing currency was a capital crime. But besides that one rather unique good – and true to the overall spirit of the country – he spied nothing in the Maenean show invented more recently than the last millennium... which seemed to defeat the purpose somewhat...

In the end, though, it didn't seem to make any difference how old and familiar or new and groundbreaking anything in the show was. Whatever diverse products and merchants were to be found – whether from Maenea, Jast-Madiir, Despotopia, or even the Twin Isles – two things remained fairly uniform: the showmanship of the vendors, and the disinterest of the browsers. For a while, this made Horus hopeful. Perhaps the show would be such a bust, Kloggem Mills would pack it in early and he could have Deborah back. But as the march lengthened, his hope steadily eroded...

Walking alongside Doctor Nokkaeru was certainly no help. Her presence provided a continuous reminder that she had once forecasted a great and sudden calamity in his life. Being suddenly bereft of Deborah felt more and more like the fulfillment of that prediction with each passing hour. Yes, it was still possible that she would do this one show and then they could get back to business as usual. But having a reason to believe she *might* be returned to his employ only seemed to make him feel worse in the aggregate, considering who that assurance had come from. And now, he had the brief encounter with the Old Heron to crown his mountain of misgivings...

All he wanted now was to see Deborah. She was supposed to be somewhere in all this commotion, and he wanted to see her... to at least be reassured that she hadn't totally vanished from existence. He was aware of becoming anxious... anxious to the point of paranoia... right when he needed to be focused...

He considered how he might further divert himself. Of the few companions available to him at the moment, he'd most prefer to talk to Miloje, but the old Deputy Constable had been quiet and thoughtful now for most of their walk. Nokkaeru was about the last person in the world he wanted to engage. That left Jether. Yes, it only made sense to talk to Jether anyway. It was clear Nokkaeru would never let them back out of the partnership now, even if neither of them had ever truly agreed to it in the first place. Horus fully expected that taking on an entry-level legal aide was going to be a good deal of trouble for him, just as he'd said it would. But at the same time, it held a glimmer of promise. He did need *someone* to externalize his thoughts to...

"So, Jether," Horus began, once he'd finally settled on an icebreaker, however weak. "I've been told you like the law."

"Yup; it's the coolest," the boy grumbled. Like any true adolescent, Jether clearly knew how to abruptly end a conversation with a bit of tasteful, biting sarcasm. Horus could think of only one way around this roadblock: honest leveling...

"That is, I've been *told* you like the law... but nothing I've heard from you would seem to confirm it."

This appeared to get through. "The law's fine, really..." Jether said at length – more earnest, but still with healthy angst. "One of the most interesting things I've researched, if I'm honest. It's just I'm over it, you know? I already learned all about the law... and all sorts of other things besides. I know everything I'd ever need to know to be placed in any skilled trade you could think of! But do my parents see that? Of course not. They just stick to their dumb old adage and treat me like a baby. They say they've never met anyone who couldn't fly that's mature enough to be trusted with anything."

Horus briefly entertained the idea of making some quip about "excepting present company," but quickly decided the exact meaning of his parents' adage was probably best left unaddressed. "So then, you're the typical boy-wonder, is that it?"

Jether looked down, kicked a stone. "Well, not *typical*, but basically... yeah. Except nobody notices. I'm ready for my own job... my own house... but they won't let me have it. They keep telling me to study more. Study *what*? Physics? Mathematics? Surgery or chemistry or economics? I've already aced it all. I've got nothing left to do with the time on my talons. So mostly, I get in trouble."

Horus wasn't greatly encouraged by this turn in the conversation, but wasn't altogether surprised, either. "What sort of trouble?"

Jether shrugged his wings. "Just perfectly harmless pranks… like secretly emptying the waste baskets or doing the laundry… or my personal favorite: waiting until no one is looking and rearranging the pantry foodstuffs from most perishable to least perishable."

Horus blinked. "Those actually *do* sound harmless."

"Yeah, well, turns out nothing is harmless around here. Grown-ups always have to have everything just-so."

"Well, how about this, then, Jether?" Horus proposed. "Why don't you come work with me on this case after all? I can't guarantee it will prove anything to your aunt, or your parents, or to grown-ups in general… but I can certainly promise you plenty of opportunities to prove something to *me*. How does that sound?"

The lad let the idea roll around in his head for a spell. "Doesn't sound like much of anything, really. But I guess I'll take it."

The two of them nodded in mutual affirmation, and Horus did find himself feeling slightly better about the whole thing.

…But like any moment of relief in recent memory, it seemed doomed to be snuffed out at once…

"Harry!" he heard, like a chorus of metal eraser stubs and nails on celestial chalkboards. "Harry, baby! You made it! You made it just in time!"

Willing himself, he turned… and sure enough, there was the dreaded person of Nostradamus Snozzwell, waving him over with boundless joy. Horus had little grounds to be quite so offended at his appearance – having walked from one side of the trade show to the other, it wasn't like he hadn't passed a score of other salesmen similarly attired, each overseeing his own carefully-devised corporate pitch. But in Horus' eyes, Snozzwell's tropical shirt would always be a little tropicaller, and his sunglasses a little sunglassier…

"I hope you're ready to witness history, Harry!" Snozzwell said as Horus and company arrived. He turned back toward a raised platform, clasping a hand on Horus' shoulder while he gestured wide across a sky filled with pie that only he had the vision to behold. "Deborah Boulevard – cereal personality extraordinaire – about to take the stage for the very first time! Can you dig it, Harry?"

"My name's not Harry," Horus explained.

"And that's not even the best part!" Snozzwell went on. "Talk about your perfect timing! Do you *know* who they say might be coming to the trade show this year?!"

He despaired to make some smart remark, but in the heat of the moment he could think of none. "I'm sure I don't."

"The Proconsul, Harry! Rumor has it the *Proconsul* might be coming, his own self! To *this* show! To *our* show! The one we're going to dominate with the help of our leading lady! Isn't that just out of this world?!"

Scarcely had he begun to privately contemplate just how much he'd like to send Snozzwell out of this world, and the sound of bugles peeled the air...

"Oh, here we go!" Snozzwell elated, pretty much jumping in place. "This is it! It's starting!"

With a final '*Bwaah*' and a rogue confetti popper, Horus' eyes locked on Deborah, who'd come to an uneasy halt at center stage. He watched her stand there in wide-eyed astonishment for glacial seconds, appearing as if she was trying to remember what to say, or why she was up there, or perhaps even her own name... and he knew at once that the stage was not her friend. He wished then that he could simply whisk her away and save her from this weirdness in true swashbuckler fashion. But legally, he had no leg to stand on. He could only look on in sympathetic agony...

Finally, Deborah produced a notecard. "Greetings from Kloggem Mills... to the investors and consumers of Roemnar," she read, a little quiet and stammery. "I...I'm Deborah Boulevard, the most famous secretary in the world." She held up a garishly colorful box. "And I'm here today to tell you about Tasty Chunks Cereal... the hip new brand that's been taking the digestive systems of Jast-Madiir by storm!"

She entertained a strategic pause here, where enthusiastic cheering had clearly been intended to go.

"...It's delicious *and* nutritious..." she claimed at length, "...made with up to 50% genuine food substitute."

Dead air reigned supreme again while a stagehand proffered Deborah a bowl and spoon, which she reluctantly accepted.

"I eat them *myself*!" she exclaimed, sounding shocked and horrified at her own assertion. "Just watch..."

They all did, with every bit of the dread-curiosity that watching someone prepare to torture themselves seemed to call for. She forced a bite, and there was a sound like real chewing, only slower...

"Mmm... *mmmmh...*" she said. The first one sounded insincere... the second, verging on a dry-heave...

At last, Horus' spirits were lifted. He didn't like watching Deborah choke down disgusting food, of course... but he couldn't help his overall relief. The exhibition was a complete train wreck. *She blew it!* he thought, unable to remember a time when he'd been more pleased. There was no way Snozzwell would opt to retain her a moment longer...

"I can't believe it," Snozzwell breathed, low and weak.

Horus smiled at him broadly, returning the favor of the shoulder-clap. "It'll be alright, Mr. Snozzwell," he said.

"*Alright*?" the salesman repeated, almost indignant. "Harry... it was magnificent!!" His arms flew out in amazement. "We've never had a better endorsement... not by a mile and half! She's a natural!"

As if on cue – while Horus strained to reconcile a single word from Snozzwell's mouth with reality – an officious Heron approached, craning up to meet the salesman...

"That was the most lackluster sales pitch I have yet witnessed in all my years," he declared.

"Yes, you see!" Horus nodded his agreement hardily toward Snozzwell. "It was painful just to watch."

"That it was," the Heron assented, before returning his own look to Snozzwell. "Your Ms. Deborah Boulevard clearly demonstrated the same disinterest in your product – and distaste for its flavor – that we would have ourselves. She has therefore set the most realistic consumer expectations that this show has ever known. And for this sole reason... I have decided to fully endorse your brand. Congratulations."

The Heron promoter walked away, leaving Horus' mouth agape.

"What'd I tell ya, Harry?" that horrible man said, giving him a friendly shake. "This is our year! This is our show! It's destiny, Harry! It's fate!"

Through all his dismay, Horus briefly caught sight of Deborah as she was being led off-stage. And, after she had quite gone, his eyes chanced to fall on Dr. Nokkaeru. He studied her for a while, processing Snozzwell's assertion. He could be right. It seemed now almost certain he *was* right. This was going to be more than some trifling speedbump on the road of his life. This was *fate*...

Chapter 9

Blucille sat stock-still at her table in the fancy, candlelit diner, not even conscious how uncharacteristic that was for her. She remained calm, composed... but alert. She turned her head slightly every so often, keeping keen eyes, ears, and nose trained on all possible angles of approach. And – somewhat more like herself – she referred back to her timepiece every so often...

The first five minutes were curious...

The next five could still comfortably be chocked-up to some comical mishap...

The ten after that seemed to suggest he'd gotten tangled in a whole string of catastrophic errors... which, given their history, was certainly plausible...

But once thirty minutes had passed, she knew there was nothing more for it. She folded her napkin back up and set it on the table, gathered her effects, and stood and left the restaurant...

* * *

"He's gone," she said, leaning with one hand and one hip on the Deputy Constable's desk. "His cover's been blown and now they've got him penned up somewhere."

Captain Alexei didn't look up from his frantic penning. Files were strewn and jumbled all across the desk – a desk that may have been a little too big for him, even if he was a foot or so taller than his boss...

"These deep cover jobs have to be improvised on the fly sometimes; you know that, Ms. Cordon," he answered dismissively. "I would not be alarmed just yet. Last we knew, he was about to infiltrate the very bowels of the Cult. That is sensitive work. I would not be at all surprised if it was some days yet before we hear from him. Now please don't trouble me further about this; I have a host of urgent matters to work through here."

"We had a date tonight and he stood me up."

Alexei flung himself from the desk in a heroic whirlwind of flying papers. "Egad! We must commence the search at once!"

* * *

Their opening move would be a sting operation on the old school building – the only firm lead they had. After some heavy debate between the DA's office and the police under Alexei's temporary administration as to the timing of the raid, it was decided to proceed that very night, rather than wait until the following morning. Blucille argued convincingly that the timely extraction of Mallard was their only realistic objective. If his cover was compromised, the ringleaders would've already gone into hiding by now. Trying to stage the sting in the morning when regular Cult meetings were common would likely result in nothing more than nabbing the small potatoes. Their best hope of catching Therodrux and his mysterious superior lay in reaching Mallard before it was too late...

Alexei and his officers eventually agreed, and Blackforest himself signed the warrant. Much as they would've preferred to save Art and end the Digit Cult all in one perfectly-timed, climatic siege on the schoolhouse, they had to accept that was likely impossible...

And so it turned out to be. They made a good show of it, of course... pouncing on the school with practically the entire SAPD, and a sizeable portion of the local garrison besides. Going in blind, and having the Czarina's standing approval to move against the Cults with extreme prejudice, there was no reason not to err on the side of overkill. But even overkill wasn't a strong enough word for it. Following the vanguard, Alexei, Blucille, and a modest escort of cops and soldiers quickly discovered the brick walls and boarded windows of the enemy stronghold concealed nothing more than empty halls. The Cults weren't just gone... they had scrubbed the place. Mallard was nowhere to be found, and the trail was dead cold...

"Ugh!" Blucille exclaimed, kicking an empty wastebasket. "We worked too hard for this! We nearly had the whole band of them by the throat! Now we've lost Therodrux! We've lost the man *over* Therodrux! And we've lost... w-we've lost..."

Unable to complete her statement, she was suddenly aware of all the sympathetic eyes on her. Her grief, anger, and embarrassment quickly proved too much...

"Oh, *Heck*... I need a puff!" she huffed, turning away and fishing soap and pipe from her pockets.

"I thought you had quite given that up," Alexei reminded her weakly.

"So did I," she replied, just before the first stream of bubbles roiled aggressively for the ceiling.

Alexei shrugged off her backsliding and returned to the business at hand. He gestured for and accepted a torch from a nearby officer, adjusting his spectacles and beginning an examination. "Well, we know they were here," he commented. "Scores of them, not long ago. Some hint or clue will have been left behind. Even the smartest criminal always neglects something. That ought to go double for a whole colony of them."

"Right," Blucille sighed, revived by Alexei's can-do spirit better and faster than the pipe. "They might've blown the place up or burnt it down... but they're just smug enough to let us have free reign of it instead. We'll make them regret it yet."

It wasn't long into their combing when they heard fast footsteps approach from the dark halls ahead of them. Alexei attended to it, finding that the captain leading the initial charge into the school had returned personally to make report...

"Captain Brocksmith," Alexei acknowledged him, each man nodding at the other. "I trust you've returned to report that you've found something."

"Quite the opposite, Sir," Brocksmith replied. "So far only empty seats and desks... a few abandoned foodstuffs in the cellar. I was just returning to suggest we bring the fire department in on the search. We ought to force open the lockers... and a few dozen men with axes could go a long way."

"Hmm..." Alexei mused, stroking thoughtfully along his sideburns. "Fire Chief Huizinga won't like it..." After a bit more silent pondering, he nodded. "Yes, a capital idea, Captain! Send word at once! And warn the messenger... the Fire Chief is a southpaw."

"Yes, sir!" Brocksmith saluted, continuing on as fast as he'd come.

"A good sport, that Brocksmith," Alexei commented. "I do believe it should've been him, leading the SAPD right now, rather than a bumpkin from Podunkville. But he respects my lead... and proffers good ideas besides."

"He brought us more than that," Blucille said.

Alexei turned and gave her a questioning look. "How so?"

"The foodstuffs in the cellar," she explained. "It's the first thing we've found that wouldn't have been here before the Cultists were."

Alexei grinned. "You think we could trace their origin? Learn something of where they get their critical supplies?"

She tapped the side of her snout. "I reckon I have the best nose for it."

"Jolly good!" the Captain exclaimed. "To the cellar!"

* * *

"Very interesting," Blucille commented, leaning over a row of airtight wooden barrels.

"I eagerly await your assessment," Alexei replied.

"Well, there's one obvious prevailing theme here," she explained as she continued down the row. "Long-term storage." She pointed at a far corner of the room. "Those are jars of honey... no mystery there." She paused over another barrel, giving a hardy sniff. "These are sealed up pretty well, but I do believe I detect a hint of apricot. This is a barrel of dried fruit, if I've ever seen one."

"You would know better than I," Alexei admitted. "Such is the fare of sailors. But we had no ports back home in Podunkville."

She sniffed another, stood up quickly. "I *really* smell this one. The wood planks are starting to warp." She moved on to yet another barrel. "But most of these are still very dry."

"What does it all add up to?"

She turned back and looked at him. "I think this is *found* food. There's no reason to buy it like this unless they were planning to go on a long trip or hunker down for a spell. But that isn't consistent with any of their plans. They want to overthrow the Czarina's administration. And in a pinch, they'd need to run, not entrench. We've seen that for ourselves."

"We've also seen their panache for repurposing old, deserted buildings," Alexei mused. "Long-term storage is the purview of the warehouse. Aren't there a few abandoned warehouses, out towards the coast?"

"A *few*?" she nearly laughed. "There're dozens! Maybe a hundred, if we don't confine ourselves to city limits."

"And we shouldn't. Certainly the Cults wouldn't concern themselves with such things."

Blucille sighed. "We need more to go on than this. Even with the garrison backing us, I don't think we can stage a raid on all the warehouses at once. Not a proper one. If we're too thinned out, they might just be able to fight back."

"And if they catch us raiding warehouses a few at a time, they could always pull up stakes again. We might end up playing a colossal game of leapfrog."

She massaged the space between her eyes. "Art might not have time for that. *Blast it*, I told him to be careful!"

Alexei came up and put an affirming hand on her shoulder. "Come now, Ms. Cordon. You've done some world-class ferreting. Why not leave the rest to the inspectors? Let's get you home, and out of this dismal cellar." For no reason he was conscious of, the captain sized-up their surroundings once again. "Though, as cellars go, this one's not so very shabby. Better-kept than our own, if truth be told."

"*Our cellar*..." Blucille thought aloud, as her mind leapt in a rogue direction. "Captain, do you remember that case Templar was working a few months back? The Inquisitor one?"

"Do I?" Alexei reeled. "Blessed be the day I could forget it! I shot the Inquisitor myself, you know."

She ignored his outburst. "I seem to recall Templar enlisting the help of... what was his name? That crackpot you keep in the basement. *Creevey*?"

"Ah yes, the graphologist," Alexei nodded his recognition. "Mr. Templar actually claimed his input was instrumental. But I fear it will be no use in our case. We've not found a single scratch of Cultist writing left behind."

She shook her head at him. "But we already have a Cultist letter... signed, stamped, and delivered straight to us!"

"By Jove!" He snapped his fingers. "The ultimatum to the Czarina! Why didn't we think of it before?"

"Simple: We weren't that desperate." Her face drew back with sudden doubt. "You have to be pretty desperate to turn to a graphologist..."

* * *

Curiously, upon their return to Civil HQ the following morning, they didn't find Creevey in the basement at all. More than that, they discovered his effects had been cleared out. After sharing a bit of a spooky moment where it seemed like anyone they tried to find had simply vanished from the face of the earth, they quickly recovered, went back upstairs and inquired about it. They soon learned that their resident graphologist had been relocated... moved to an office on the first floor...

"Well, good morning, Captain, Ms. Cordon!" Milt Lias Creevey greeted them boisterously, looking very pleased indeed to see them as he turned away from the beautiful vista of his nice big window. "I have to admit, I almost feel underdressed," he laughed. "Imagine an Assistant District Attorney and the acting Deputy Constable walking into my humble lodgings this fine morning. How can I help?"

Alexei didn't answer right away, choosing instead to cast a questioning look all around the room. "This was Sergeant Ruso's office, last I knew," he said. "I'm surprised to see it change hands."

"Pavel took Sergeant Turketski's office after his promotion," Dr. Creevey explained. "He was kind enough to offer me his."

The Captain appeared unconvinced. "Strange. I understood this to be the most coveted office on the floor. I wonder why Ruso would give it up."

Creevey threw up his hands. "Who can account for a man's charity? Chock it up to a personal favor, if you must. That's how I framed it."

"Hmm," Alexei said, remaining ponderous. He studied the smile on Creevey's face... finding it much too authentic not to be suspicious...

...But then, maybe it was just the goatee...

"Well never mind," Blucille finally intervened. She produced the ultimatum with a ruffle and a crinkle and slapped it on his desk. "Here's our business. What do you make of it?"

"There's the Blucille Cordon I know... straight to brass tacks," Creevey commented appreciatively as he gathered both letter and loupe to himself. "Let's see what we have here."

They watched him scan the note... and scan it... and *scan* it... leaning closer as he went, until the loupe nearly scratched the paper. He started over – more frantic, more tense. He gave it a third read. And then, he sat up. He looked horrified...

"I can't read it," he admitted, is if to a ghost.

Blucille waved her hand dismissively and let it drop to her side. "That figures!" She turned away and clenched her fists. "I should've *known* this would be a stupid waste of time!"

"Now see here, Dr. Creevey!" Alexei demanded sternly. "We have a potential insurrection on our hands, and a good man's life may be at stake! This is no time to come up blank. At least give us something in keeping with your profession. Tell us Therodrux's mother's name... or his favorite ice cream flavor... or some odd thing! I don't much care how zany or innocuous. But you must let us have *something* to work with!"

"You don't understand," Creevey appealed, shaking his head. "The way this man wrote the letter – every small hand movement, every stroke of the pen – it's completely incomprehensible! Total, subtextual gibberish!"

"Baloney," Blucille replied, leveling a fairly scalding expression at him. "I've read that letter myself and it was *very* clear. Therodrux could hardly have been more to the point, outlining his expectations for the Czarina. I grant the demands themselves were insane... but the language used to convey them certainly was not."

"You're still not getting it," Creevey answered darkly, standing and leaning over his desk, seeming now much less in awe of his callers than he'd made out at the start. "I don't care a lick about the words. I'm talking about the *man*. I can't read anything about the *man*! It's like his brain's been taken all apart and thrown back together!"

Alexei and Blucille made no reply. They stood for a while, quiet and contemplative. It seemed that even finding nothing at all had given them something to think about...

"You mean to say that Therodrux's mind is somehow altered beyond recognition?" Alexei tried musing aloud. "That his thought-patterns are now jumbled and disorderly beyond recognition?"

"Worse than that," Dr. Creevey boded. "They're actually *too* orderly." He picked the ultimatum up and waved it at them. "Plying graphology to this letter is like trying to put together a psychological profile for a typewriter! The man's practically a machine!"

"Preposterous!" Alexei challenged. "Surely you're making some excuse... however elaborate. The ringleader of the Cults would certainly need the power of independent thought."

"No," Blucille interjected, even more lost in thought. "Art himself said Therodrux was just another cog." She worked to recall his words. "'An unnatural talent for persuasion'. That's how Art characterized their true leader..." She looked up at Creevey again, resolute. "Is it possible for one person to deprogram another? To get into their heads and mess things up... to condition them to think what you want them to think... even believe what you want them to believe?"

Creevey seemed to shrink from this question, holding up defensive hands. "That's a bit outside my realm of expertise."

"Then what's your opinion? Do you think it *might* be possible?"

Creevey set his jaw, rubbed his goatee. "Mind you, I've never seen it done... but I've heard rumors. Whispers, you might say. There's even a word for what you're talking about. They call it... *hypnosis*."

Alexei and Cordon exchanged anxious glances. "I do wonder if we've learned something of our enemy's means here," Alexei said.

She nodded. “I don’t doubt we have.”

“But what of the search? Where do we go from here?”

“I don’t know,” she admitted. “We’ve lost the scent.”

“We’ll find it again,” he assured her. “We have to.”

“In more ways than one,” she agreed. “I’m afraid Art’s in worse danger than we thought...”

Chapter 10

Horus kept his pace good and brisk, grocery bag crunching under his arm like a papery sail in a windstorm, while he reflected on his trip to the meat market. It wasn't the boost he'd hoped it would be. Herons turned out to be even worse about letting food mature than Humans. He'd found only one item in the shop that looked distressed enough to really rouse his appetite, but when he learned that it was pediatric food, and had a moment to reflect on the true meaning of the label 'Pre-Processed', he decided to settle on the oldest Hypsilophodon haunch he could find...

And now, he was jogging. He had the best cut of meat he was likely to find in Roemnar and he was jogging. Anything he could think of to stay loose – to get the brain juices flowing – to generally feel alert and positive – he aimed to busy himself with such things for the next few hours. He needed to be in prime shape, and he wasn't going to let anything slow him down. Not today...

...Day One of the Berlie Beirel case...

He could feel the exercise and the relatively fresh air doing its good work. He was invigorated. He was sure of himself...

Then, he reached his bungalow. He hopped to a stop in his tracks. He blinked while his mouth-breathing face slowly contorted. Naturally, some sort of shenanigans had started-up in the short time he was out. He watched incredulous while a group of postmen wheeled heavy-looking parcels into his place on little trucks...

At length, he shook himself and proceeded on, struggling to wedge himself through the channel around the building without getting much in their way. The tiny Phage postal workers were too diligent in their work to take much notice of him, nor did he bother to ask them what they were doing. He had some sense the answer was waiting inside...

Sure enough, once he stood pressed up against the trench opposite the doorway, he quickly identified someone within who'd better have a good explanation. There – in the living space by the back walls – was Jether, directing the unloading of the trucks. Stacks of boxes were now cluttered around his dining room. His place was in chaos and commotion, and he didn't have the slightest notion why...

Finally, finding an opening between workmen coming and going, he let himself in. He approached slowly, deliberately – as mature people are wont to do when wading into the fruits of teenage initiative. He quite expected his boy-wonder aide to notice him at once and come volunteer that explanation he'd better have. But after several paces, he grew too weary of feeling overlooked...

"Jether!" he called. "Come here a moment, would you?"

"Oh, hi, Mr. Templar," Jether replied, fluttering up to him. "What's up?"

"What indeed," he quipped, suppressing a bit of temper. "Jether... would you mind very much explaining this... mass drop?"

"Well, the other day when my aunt brought me over, I couldn't help noticing that your walls weren't covered in case reports. The whole home library was totally empty! Obviously a lawyer can't be expected to work in a void. So I arranged to have all these delivered."

"Case reports?" Horus asked.

"Yeah!" Jether smartly lanced a nearby box open with a talon and fished out a big hard-bound volume. "See? Just what you needed, right?"

"Jether," Horus started again, rubbing a hand down his face. "This is a thoughtful gesture... but rather unnecessary. I have *Vilkerracht* with me and a few select case reports already."

"Pfft, *Vilkerracht*?" Jether asked, sounding like he'd been told a bad joke. "Come on, Mr. Templar, are you serious? What's *Vilkerracht* next to even a dozen volumes of case reports from real international trials? You're a big-picture guy, aren't you? Why consult a little doodle when what you really need is a whole fresco!"

Horus took stock of all the boxes piling up. "This looks like more than a dozen volumes to me."

"Oh, it is," Jether assured him enthusiastically. "I ordered everything I could round up... not just on the international cases, but collections from each individual state connected with this thing. Cases from your own Jast-Madiir; cases from Roemnar, since that's where we are. Unfortunately I had to special-order the reports from Tophthaera; no one had them in stock. But they should be here in 11 to 25 weeks."

"*I* won't be here in 11 to 25 weeks," Horus reminded him, gently as he could. "Jether, I can see how this would be an exemplary resource... given unlimited time. But in case you've forgotten, the trial starts *today*. There's time for a good meal..." he reviewed the present accessibility of his dining room furnishings, "... at best. And then we'll be off to the Annex Tribunal. We don't even have time to put all these books on the shelf, much less read them."

"No problem," Jether claimed. "I'm sure the shipping guys will take care of that."

"No, we won't," a shipping guy interjected. "We deliver the parcels. That is our solemn charge. It would be tantamount to heresy if we were to open and handle their contents."

"Oh, but what if we paid you more?" Jether asked, a bit whiney.

"To betray our oaths and deep convictions?" the Phage replied, indignant. "May Heck itself strike down such a notion!"

Horus shook his head. "Really Jether, I'm surprised you can even afford to have all these books delivered in the first place."

"Oh, I don't have any money," the young Heron informed him. "I told them to bill you."

"...I see," Horus replied, postulating his odds of affording groceries for the remainder of the stay, or any time within the next calendar year. It left very little room in his mind for that precious positivity he'd jogged so hard for, dimly as he could now recall the experience...

* * *

CRUNCH

Horus took another bite of dino haunch... one more than he'd meant to, as he'd resolved to ration the rest. It was still basically frozen, but he had no time to wait for Jether to unbury the stove he might've used to thaw it out. "So, you weren't able to get a list of the prosecution witnesses?" he asked once he'd chewed most of the bite, hoping he wasn't also chewing cracked bits of his own teeth.

"*Able*, maybe," the youth answered, setting another book on the shelf. "I didn't feel much like asking. Grown-ups always get upset when you ask them for things."

"Well, you're going to have to be more assertive in the future," Horus sighed. "They have no grounds to restrict our access." He looked back at Jether, noticing too late that the lad was putting the books up in an order that seemed completely random. "Those reports are numbered, you know," he pointed out.

"Yeah," he replied dismissively. "I'm using the Dudley Decimal System."

"That might be all well and good," Horus claimed, scratching under his chin, "...if I were a librarian. I think it would be better to just have them in numeric order."

"Okay," Jether recited distantly. Then, after a moment's hesitation, he put another book on the shelf in just the same fashion he had been...

Brimming with internal combustion, Horus just pressed his eyes shut and returned to his own business. He set the haunch on an unburied part of the table and went for his briefcase, already open.

"I trust you finished filling out those waivers I started, at least," Horus called over his shoulder, feeling the word 'trust' to be quite stretched here.

"I did," Jether answered. Horus found and retrieved the waivers at about the same time, nodding with approval as he discovered the fields really were all filled-in...

"Impressive," he commented. "I have to say I'm actually quite pleased with your work here."

"Well now, don't make a snap-judgment, Mr. Templar," Jether warned him. "Of course, my work is top-notch. But that doesn't change the fact that you need to *check* it... that's part of your duty as a mentor. In fact, I figured you'd get too secure in my accuracy, so I made a few mistakes in there on purpose. They're subtle, so you may want to check my work in triplicate."

Horus shook his head again, returning the papers to his case for the time being. "I begin to wonder which of us is really the secretary."

"That's easy... neither one. I'm your aide, remember?"

"Of course... and how very aided I feel." Horus shut his case with exaggerated gusto and snatched it up from the table. "Come now, Jether. It's time to go."

* * *

The doors came open at their approach... apparently on their own. The armed men barring the way only raised their spears for Horus and Jether to pass. No mere bailiffs, these were royal Centurions – the Proconsul's men... easily the most rigorously trained and effective killers in this part of the world. Horus gulped as he crossed the threshold into the court chambers – an angular enclosure, rather like a sharply-chiseled hourglass in overall shape. Very tall. Very moody... with meager light like that of a stormy sky coming from far, far above...

Walking into the chamber's midst, his sight was naturally drawn upwards in search of the Viziers – the trifecta of presiding judges who made up the Tribunal – the highest echelon of arbiters in the Archipelago. A few stories up, they each had their own private alcove in three pale, adjoining walls, where they sat silent in the shadows. There was no sound in all the vast enclosure but what Horus presently made as he ventured forward. Each little footstep seemed loud and rude in this place of great and glorious condescension. Being a part of all this, he yearned to cut through the belittling atmosphere and reassure himself. He let his eyes rest on the nook of Rashida Neferib for a while. She'd officiated *Jast Madiir vs. The Mantid* earlier that same year, so at least he'd met her before... and even had good reason to suspect she remembered him. He dared grin and nod her way. In true impassive form, she made no sign of her own. Horus' nerves were not greatly eased...

Turning away as he neared the center of the room, he looked back whence he'd come. Lofted above the entryway were steep rows of motionless onlookers – most or all of them resident Herons. Horus wondered at their presence. It was no jury trial he was stepping into. The rulings of the Annex Tribunal were arbitrated by the consensus of the Viziers alone. These people could only be spectators... the common clay of Roemnar, rounded up to fill the seats. Even so, the steely look they gave him over their long, sharp beaks told him they were no less capable of being judgmental...

"Ho there, Mr. Templar, Sir!" a shockingly unreserved voice greeted him. "Very good to see you again, it is! We 'ad only that one brief parley some days ago, and I confess I began to feel you'd plum forgotten about lil' old me. Oh, but I know you've been busy!"

Horus turned slowly on his footpad. In the awe of the place, he'd walked unwittingly almost straight to his client, shackled to the floor before the judges...

"Yes... hello, Mo..." he replied, all terse whispers and a nervous smile, feeling every ounce of the towering gaffe that his client was apparently oblivious to. "I am sorry I've been out-of-touch, but rest assured things are being handled..."

"I don't doubt it, Sir, not one bit! Yer an 'onest fellow, I can see!" Mo flashed exuberantly. "An' who might this lil' friend of yours be? I've not met 'im yet!"

"I'm Jether – Mr. Templar's legal aide," Jether announced himself with similar abandon. "Nice to meet you."

"Mighty pleased to meet you as well, Sir!" Mo bobbed in the air.

"This might not be the ideal time to discuss it..." Horus forced through his teeth.

"Indeed it is not," Vizier Arcturus declared, rising from his seat while his voice beat against the walls. "The accused and his council have been gathered. Let the trial of *Mobipetrolluck vs. The States* commence." He struck with a steel gavel... a truly piercing sound.

And so it was officially begun... *Mobipetrolluck vs. The States*: a case whose very name had been the subject of some squabble and scandal. Originally to be called "Mobipetrolluck vs. Tophthera vs. Toefthaera," Asiri's administration formally petitioned against being mentioned last. Of course, the representatives of the North would only have protested the same if the order had simply been reversed. In the end, "the States" was a welcome concession to both, acknowledging the sovereignty of two nations that had formerly been one...

But as to the respective attorneys of "the States," they were presently nowhere to be found...

"Where are the prosecutors?" Jether whispered up at Horus, noticing as much.

"That's not for me to say," Horus snapped back hoarsely. "Keep quiet."

"Well I just don't see how you're supposed to do this without them," the boy insisted. "Someone should be alerted."

Horus was beside himself. "Do you honestly think the Viziers haven't noticed?! What kind of...?!"

"The defense will refrain from its outbursts," Arcturus cautioned. "Let the prosecution and the prosecution come forth! Let them present their cases!"

All gathered attended once again to the entryway. Soon enough, two sharply-dressed Meduselda floated into the chamber – one appearing rather squat, the other tall and oblong. Though he did not yet know which was from where, Horus was relieved to see there would be an easy visual cue to tell them apart...

Once beyond the narrow channel leading into the court, the two prosecutors parted ways in apparently practiced synchronous, circling in on Mo from both sides of the room...

The remaining Viziers stood. "The seeking parties will declare themselves in clockwise order, beginning with the Defense," Neferib announced.

"Horus Templar of Jast-Madiir," Horus complied.

"Demicolon of Tophthera," said the prosecutor on his left – the taller one. The tone of his speech was deep and indomitable.

"Pseudofluff of Toefthaera," the shorter prosecutor on his right declared. His voice was scratchy and subsumed, but boasted of a crafty intelligence. Horus had a hard time reading their inflections – especially since the names of both countries sounded exactly the same when spoken aloud – but after careful consideration, he understood that Demicolon was of the North, and Pseudofluff from the South.

"What are the charges brought against this drone, Mobipetrolluck?" the third Vizier – Serapis – inquired.

"The defendant floats accused of two counts of Draft Evasion," Demicolon explained.

"One from each of our respective states," Pseudofluff qualified.

"And how does the defendant plea?"

Mo began to pipe up, finally seeming healthily alarmed and diminished by it all. He stammered only a few short nothings before Horus interrupted him...

"If the Court please, the defense contends that no applicable charges have been brought against my client."

Vizier Arcturus leveled a cautioning finger at Horus. "Even if that is so, procedure demands you venture a plea of not guilty for the time being. The Court will entertain the defense's case after those of the prosecutions. You are out of order, Counselor."

"Wait a minute," Vizier Neferib appealed. "The defense has its right to an opening statement." Finally, she looked on Horus with some of the familiarity he'd been hoping for. "I may have been in error to waive that right once before. If Councilor Templar is truly prepared to demonstrate the inadmissibility of the prosecutions' case, we may save ourselves a good deal of trouble."

Arcturus was darkly thoughtful. "I would remind my esteemed colleague to refrain from personalities. But very well; the defense may present an opening statement."

Horus nodded, feeling a surge of confidence. "The defense respectfully begins with an obvious fact: We are here to resolve a matter of citizenship. A question, your Honors: Does any state have the right to conscript a man who is *not* in fact a citizen of said state?"

The Viziers exchanged glances. "No such right has ever been upheld, to our knowledge," Serapis answered on their behalf.

Horus quickly and deftly reached into his briefcase, producing a document. "I have here, in my hand, Mobipetrolluck's certification of citizenship in the country of Jast-Madiir." He shot a squinty look at each of his rivals. "What do the prosecutions intend to present in return? Where are the documents certifying his citizenship in Tophthera or Toefthaera? I tell you now: There are no such certifications! My client predates the existence of both states and has never set tentacle above either one of them!" He looked up again at the judges. "I concede that his first allegiance was to the now-defunct parent state of Tophthaera, which might've rightly conscripted him. But these men and their respective countries have no claim."

The room was quiet for a while – thoughtful. "The defense's point is indeed well-taken," Arcturus admitted at length. "How would the prosecutions answer?"

"Quite simply," Pseudofluff answered, venomously undeterred. "Mr. Templar makes his case with skillfully chosen words. He is careful to appeal to matters of 'citizenship' and 'nationality'. He wisely avoids mention of his client's *Dominion*, from which the very concept of nations traces its origin."

"The drone Mobipetrolluck is a *Berlie Beirel*," Demicolon asserted, ambling at Horus. "Is that not so, Counselor? Or, would you try to deny it?"

Horus swallowed hard again, feeling surrounded. "On the contrary – the obvious facts force me to stipulate. He *is* a Berlie Beirel."

"Well said," Demicolon bobbed in a nodding fashion. "And as such, he is subject to the *Queen* of the Berlie Beirels – the very one who has demanded his service."

"*She* is his master, by birthright," Pseudofluff went on. "So it is, and has ever been."

Horus shook his head. "But *his* Queen was Yeminéya – the one who came before Asiri and Irisa. She bore him. And now, her days as his master have passed. She's gone."

"Do you think your client is unique in this?" Pseudofluff asked. "Would you suppose he is the only drone to ever outlive his first Queen?"

"Many of us do," Demicolon explained. "But the Queen who succeeds her inherits all the authority due her station. I assure you: Mobipetrolluck's master is alive and well."

"And who precisely would that be?" Horus demanded, embracing the question, whether for better or worse.

"Order!" Arcturus commanded. He sat, rubbing his temples. "We seem to have regressed very quickly into open forum. The rebuttal of the prosecutions is revealing: I don't doubt you mean to introduce this side business of resolving your Dominion's internal politics. Let me speak clearly on behalf of this Tribunal: We have come to reach arbitration on the sole case of this drone. We are *not* here to name one of your Queens the rightful inheritor of Berlie Beireldom!"

"With respect, most esteemed Viziers," Demicolon appealed, "right of succession is the unavoidable heart of the matter." At this juncture, he and Pseudofluff each produced a document of their own. "Behold, prosecution exhibit-A and prosecution exhibit-A. Photostats of Mobipetrolluck's conscription orders. Each orderly and officious. Each apparently valid and binding. And yet, the defendant cannot possibly answer them both."

"Not simultaneously, at any rate," Pseudofluff qualified.

"Indubitably," his counterpart agreed. "One state – one *Queen* – must be awarded priority in this contentious matter."

"The mandate of these orders must be weighed... one against the other... and a victor chosen."

"There is no alternative."

"If it please the Court," Horus interjected into their villainous dialoguing. "My colleagues have duly pointed out that it would be impossible for my client to serve in both the northern and southern armies simultaneously. May I suggest that it is the very implausibility of simultaneous action which could hold the key to awarding priority."

"How so, Counselor?" Serapis asked.

"Wait," Arcturus cut in. "Lest he forget, Mr. Templar is not here to mediate between the prosecutions and the Court. His duty is to refute *both* damaging claims against his client, not to help us to decide which to enforce, or in what order."

"Never mind, your Honors," Pseudofluff volunteered. "Mr. Templar hastens us toward a matter of clarification that we have anticipated... and prepared for."

"What matter!?" Serapis demanded. "You're all talking around something that presently eludes me. I should like to know where Mr. Templar is allegedly hastening us."

"Go ahead, Counselor," Neferib invited Horus. "Explain your point about simultaneous action."

Horus folded his hands behind his back. "Perhaps I did begin to speak out of turn before. Nevertheless, I find it implausible that two summons from two separate countries could have been issued at the same time. Defense stipulates that they were received on the same day. Defense even stipulates that they were opened and read at the same time. As much was admitted in deposition. But surely one or the other of these orders was *mailed* first."

"This is a point worthy of investigation," Neferib argued to her peers. "And I suspect this is the time to do it. The prosecutors are to make their cases first. Let them begin by shedding what light they can on the order of events leading up to the alleged crimes."

"Agreed," Arcturus replied. "As agents of the states that issued the summons, the burden of reconstructing a timeline rests with them."

Horus was privately elated at this turn. An inquiry into the exact mailing date of the draft notices could delay proceedings for weeks. That would give Mo quality time to enjoy the privileges Horus had been scheming to arrange for him since the earliest days of their voyage to Roemnar. It was really no surprise that the Viziers were quick to support such an inquest... from Blackforest's brief alone, Horus had good reason to suspect they would be willing to go to almost any length to avoid ruling in favor of one Queen or the other solely on the grounds of their own merits. Still, he was greatly pleased to see his strategy go over without a hitch...

"It is well," Demicolon replied, sounding very much that he meant it. Horus' confidence began to wither. "Let it be as you say. For as Mr. Pseudofluff has already mentioned, this is a point for which we've carefully prepared..."

"The prosecutions stand ready to call their first witness," Pseudofluff announced.

There was a moment of deliberation. "The two of you mean to call one witness to testify on behalf of... *both* your cases?" Serapis asked.

"Oh yes," Pseudofluff assured him. "It suits our present purposes quite well."

"Then let the witness be called," Serapis assented, sounding a bit like a man stepping into a trap. Horus felt the same...

"We call his eminence, Rutherford Cortez D'Allemagne, Postmaster General of Idriulthoronta."

Horus turned back to the entrance once more, breathless to behold a surprise witness of such prominence. Sure enough, a tiny little Phage in a flowing fur-lined cape tinked forth on the ends of his five miniscule legs, filling the chamber with all the brilliant stateliness of a great king, long-absent, finally coming into his own... and not much liking what he found there. He paused at the threshold, adjusting his monocle with an arresting sort of disdain. And then, he crossed into the Tribunal...

* * *

"We show you now these photostats of summons mailed to a one Mobipetrolluck at his residence in Jast-Madiir," Demicolon narrated to the court, as he and Pseudofluff held out summons to an impassive Postmaster.

"Are these documents known to you?" Pseudofluff asked.

The General did not answer at once, his polyhedral head turning down on them from his booster seat behind the witness stand. "They are known to me. And where they should *not* be."

"You were present for their processing, were you not?" Demicolon pressed him.

"I was. I witnessed the application of the postmark, the stamp, and the envelope." He paused, forcing himself through a particularly distasteful point. "I was even made to witness the drafting of the letters themselves." His voice was an odd mingling of remorse and accusation.

"And which letter would you say was the first to be postmarked?"

"To be stamped?"

"To be enveloped?"

"To be written?"

"Objection!" Horus called. "The prosecutors are badgering their witness. Let them give him a chance to answer each question before proceeding to the next."

"It's quite alright, Counselor," General Rutherford interjected. "Well these men know the snare they have set. I resent my part in it deeply; nevertheless I am constrained to the truth. In each case – to all questions – the answer is the same: Neither letter was first. Each was penned, processed, and postmarked in perfect synchronous. Down to the very millisecond."

The Meduseldan attorneys flashed brightly with devious triumph. Horus was dumbfounded at this turn. Fixing searching eyes up at the Viziers, he only made things worse for himself, seeing that they all appeared equally astonished. *Blackforest warned they'd be prepared for this*, he thought to himself. *And **how** they've prepared! But surely they can't just... they can't be allowed to just...*

"Your Honors!" Horus appealed. He froze in his own outburst. He was out of order...

"Yes, Mr. Templar?" Arcturus asked.

His ears folded back; he felt very foolish. "Forgive me, your Honors. I merely meant to petition for my right to cross examine this witness."

"You certainly may," Arcturus granted, sounding notably relieved that Horus meant to cross examine. "But let us not get ahead of ourselves. The prosecutions must first finish direct examination."

"No matter, your Honors," Demicolon said, as he and Pseudofluff floated away from the stand. "It *is* finished. The defense may exercise his privilege."

After the prosecutors had passed him by, Horus adjusted his collar and took their place by the stand. "Now, General... my colleagues have just introduced some rather shocking testimony. Certainly no less shocking, considering the weight it carries... coming from one as elevated as yourself."

"Please, Mr. Horus Templar, do not patronize me," the General sighed. "I am only a flawed creation, as any other. Would that you could impeach my testimony and free me from my part in this dreadful conspiracy. Alas! What I have said is true, and can be confirmed by other witnesses of stout character."

Horus stroked his jowls thoughtfully. "I note your repeated reference to a 'trap' or 'conspiracy'; I confess that something in all this does seem horribly amiss. Surely it is not expected of you to oversee the postmarking of each individual letter and mailer throughout the Archipelago?"

"Indeed not. Nor do I lightly set my vision on the contents of personal correspondence! To us, this is a deadly grievous thing." His monocle turned on the other attorneys, who finally and duly shrunk under its shimmer. "But these drones came one day skulking into our central office, entangling us in we knew not what. They appealed to us – most curiously – that they had special need... a pair of documents which must be mailed in simultaneity. We could not guess at their purposes, but in goodwill agreed to accommodate them. And it was by that very spirit of goodwill that they bound us over to wickedness. Requests merely curious were soon followed by bold and callous ones. They demanded..." the General faltered. "They insisted that the documents required *witnesses* to be proper and binding! They were politely invited to find their witnesses elsewhere, for we are charged never to break the sacred confidence – to look upon one's mail. But they would not be moved. They were *incorrigible*. They even went as far as accusing us of obstructing their right to our services!

"Word reached to me of this disruption, and I went down to the sorting room myself so to rectify things. I explained our position at great length, but still they would not relent. I watched a number of my best men and women chafe under the moral dilemma these drones hemmed us into for hours, until at last it proved too much. Some volunteered to accept the disgrace of witnessing the letters, if only to fulfill the higher calling of delivering them to their rightful recipient. But I would not have it. Rather, I accepted the disgrace myself – I, and two of my Lieutenants, for these drones would settle on no less than three witnesses. I see now that this was part of their design from the first – to procure my testimony. These scalawags took the very best of our virtues and turned them inside-out... and in so doing, they now bind your own estimable selves to their malicious purposes. I am sorely used. I am ashamed."

He paused here, his gaze cast at the ground. But then, he looked on Demicolon and Pseudofluff again, with a different aspect in his monocle altogether... "Yet even such as these should know... their mail is always welcome within our post offices. It will be handled with no less care. It will be cherished with solemnity undimmed."

Horus was slow to remember himself, having been quite carried away with General Rutherford's pained and potent soliloquy. He looked up at the judges, who were also moved. "Your Honors," he began low. "We see now the underhanded dealings of these agents unmasked. It is with a heavy heart that I must move to have Mr. Demicolon and Mr. Pseudofluff bound over on charges of tampering with evidence."

"And how would you contrive that we tampered with evidence, Mr. Templar?" Demicolon asked. "We authored duly witnessed draft orders, fully empowered to do so by our respective states." He shrugged a sly shrug. "We made certain *special requests* of the Post, none of which are restricted by any legal language, whether national or international."

"To refer to the draft orders themselves in the given time and setting as 'evidence' is a fallacy," Pseudofluff continued. "There was no crime until Mobipetrolluck's alleged evasion of said orders... evasion we did nothing to incite. The defendant's reaction to the drafts were of his own will and accord. We did nothing illegal, nor did we force anyone else into illegal activity."

"Didn't you?" Horus challenged. "Perhaps you can sidestep tampering with evidence... but how about *entrapment*? You railroaded my client into making an impossible decision. Any one order he answered would have made him liable to charges of draft evasion from the other order!"

"So it would appear, on the surface," Demicolon replied. "But you forget... both orders assert the full weight and authority of the Queen of the

Berlie Beirels... the one, *true* Queen of the Berlie Beirels. Mobipetrolluck had but to enlist his own best judgment, and determine which of the Queens was indeed his rightful master. Yet he failed to do so."

"Which brings us again to the real heart of the matter," Pseudofluff segued. "We must determine which Queen is owed Mobipetrolluck's service, and which is not. All other things – most assuredly – having been determined quite equal."

Horus only blinked. His opponents had entered into a bald-faced conspiracy to orchestrate and subsequently hijack an international incident in the region's highest court, and there was nothing he could do to prevent them getting away with it. Judging by the painful silence of the room, there was nothing that even the great Viziers could do about it...

"Does the defense have any further questions for this witness?" Arcturus fairly pleaded.

"Not at this time, your Honor," Horus admitted, his shoulders and gut all in a droop.

The Viziers remained quiet for a spell, no doubt hoping some other question would come to Horus belatedly. "The witness may step down," they allowed at length. Arcturus closed his eyes hard, pressing fingers into the side of his wearied head as Rutherford departed. "How now do the prosecutions intend to proceed?"

"The next phase is clear, your Honors," Pseudofluff asserted. "We must each present our case for our Queen. We must establish priority – one over the other. Only then can the defendant's sentencing be duly decided and carried out."

"You wish to begin introducing evidence of Asiri's sole Queenship over the Berlie Beirels?"

"Yes," Pseudofluff answered.

"And I for Irisa," Demicolon was quick to make known.

"Very well," Arcturus sighed. "We will give each of you a full court session to present his arguments. No more! This Tribunal will not be cornered into an endless debate. We will hear the arguments of Mr. Pseudofluff at our next convening, followed by Mr. Demicolon on the following court day."

"Objection!" Pseudofluff called, just before Arcturus could strike his gavel. They all looked at him quizzically. "I vehemently protest to being heard first! Why should the arguments of my opponent be fresher in the minds of your Honors when sentencing is carried?"

"Nor should Asiri be awarded the honor of first recognition by your graces!" Demicolon argued. "That in itself is a matter of precedent, which she certainly has not earned."

Arcturus turned away, needing a moment. Serapis took over...

"So then... you don't wish to be first, and you don't wish to be second," he said, looking to each in turn. "I don't suppose that we could simply hear you in the reverse order, and that would clear everything up?"

"Unconscionable!" Demicolon exclaimed.

"Absolutely not!" Pseudofluff agreed heartily.

Serapis also resigned to a moment of private council.

"What then would the prosecutions propose *instead*?" Neferib demanded, her own voice cracking somewhat. "How can we equitably overcome this deadlock?"

Demicolon and Pseudofluff conferred for a while, having apparently come to a part of their scheme which they hadn't hashed-out quite so much. Their whispers carried far, but managed to remain indistinct... rather a feat, in a room that seemed designed to capture and amplify all speech. Finally, they must've reached some new stroke of brilliance. They broke sidebar and addressed the court...

"We request to present our arguments at the same time," Demicolon stated.

Neferib winced. "Both of you at once? To open court?" she asked, hoping against hope that there was some misunderstanding.

"Yes," Pseudofluff answered. "It is the only way to give our cases the fair consideration they deserve."

The Viziers all looked to one another. "At least it's expedient," Serapis put forth. "We can have it over in a single day."

Arcturus nodded. "Very well then. The prosecutions will present their cases, beginning at 9:00 tomorrow. Court is adjourned until then." He struck his steel gavel.

Horus let out a long breath, searching the floor blankly for answers. The issue of the Queens the Tribunal meant to avoid above all else had come upon them inevitably... and for all his cleverness, Horus himself had done his part to steer the case onto those very dreaded tracks. The choice ahead of them could have unfathomable implications...

But he had to remind himself... his primary concern was his client. Perhaps there was still a way to ensure Mo a light sentence and a speedy return to his beloved Clerking duties. Yes, above all else, he needed to grant

Mo *some* victory. He needed to prove goodwill. And he needed to do it *here*, where word of his deeds would carry furthest. He still had his good example to set. That was his highest objective, and it may yet be attainable...

"Mr. Templar, Sir!" Mo called, Horus being so lost in his own thoughts, he'd nearly walked out without a word. "Pardon my asking, Sir, but what becomes of me now? I'm afraid, in all the tension – and my not being much for legalese – well, it all rather flew over me, in a manner o' speaking."

Horus was presently torn – he saw his client needed some reassurance, but now seemed the inopportune time. He needed to withdraw and strategize. And he was *this close* to having some news for Mo that was worth all the uneasy waiting...

"Regrettably, you must return to your cell for now," he explained, even as he backpedaled. "Nothing has been decided as yet. But don't despair! I expect you will have a good deal of your livelihood restored to you very soon!"

Mo flashed with bewilderment. "I... I'm not sure I understand, Sir!"

Horus checked his timepiece, growing anxious at being held up from the critical business that lay ahead of him. "I'll explain it in the morning before court! Hold onto your hope in the meantime, Mo! We'll come out ahead of this yet!" He waved goodbye.

"If y' say so, Sir," Mo's voice reached him weakly...

* * *

"Those guys were awesome," Jether said, alight with juvenile enthusiasm as they made their way back towards the surface. "They pretty much walked all over you! Even the Viziers and General Rutherford himself couldn't touch 'em. They had everybody eating out of the palm of their tentacle! It was incredible! In all my studies, I never imagined just how cool the law could be."

"Well, at least one of us enjoyed himself," Horus sighed while they marched through the busy halls. "Hamilton warned me this would be a battle, and I prepared for one... or, so I thought. We're really going to have to dig-in our dew claws now, Jether. Our client, the good name of the legal system, and justice at large depend on it."

"Just promise me one thing, Mr. Templar."

"What's that?"

"Promise me that when you lose, you'll show me how to lose classy. I think I'll learn everything I need to know about *winning* classy from watching Mr. Demicolon and Mr. Pseudofluff."

Horus shook his head. "I'm not about to..."

"...Horus!"

He was cut-off midsentence by a familiar butterscotch voice with a deep but feminine musical sweetness. It brought him to a grinding halt, nearly causing him to trip over his own feet as he searched for the source...

"*Deborah,*" he confirmed, probably too noticeably awed...

"Hi," she said, fixing a weak smile on her face for only a fleeting moment. They stood together now in the hall. But after sharing a mere second or two, it was immediately apparent she was in a fret to be gone again. "I'm sorry there's no time," she explained. "I couldn't get away quick enough to make the trial... and now I've already lingered too long. But I wanted you to know I *tried* to be here. And I'm going to try again tomorrow. I can't promise I'll make the 9:00 cutoff, but we might have a proper minute afterwards to catch up. I really will make an effort."

He nodded solemnly, feeling a sort of humble, honored anguish. "Of course. I couldn't ask for more. Thank you, Deborah."

She kneaded her own hands as she began to step away. "Well, I really have to be off now. Later, Boss," she managed.

"Goodbye..." he replied, surely much too softly...

And just like that, she was gone again.

"Was that your secretary?" Jether asked.

"Yes," Horus answered.

Jether nodded. "She seems nice. And she's a very famous person. You should marry her."

"Jether..." Horus began, looking down on the boy-wonder, "...you have a lot of growing up to do."

"Or maybe *some people* are just too grown-up," the youth bit back.

After such an ambush, little did Horus suspect he would be cut-off on his way out of the Tribunal Complex a second time. But just as they were coming to the exit, a couple of Meduselda – one in a violet uniform, and the other in deep blue – floated up in their way... fairly *barred* them. Horus quickly intuited that these were military attachés assisting his courtroom foils. What they had to say for themselves confirmed as much...

"You are Horus Templar, we presume? Attorney Pseudofluff would like a word with you," the drone in violet explained.

"As would Attorney Demicolon," the other added. Horus was growing quite used to the pattern...

"And, if we refuse?" Horus challenged. "Have the two of them so thoroughly subverted the Annex Tribunal that you would dare to enforce their wishes here?"

The attachés exchanged a look. "We don't mean to threaten you, Counselor – only convey their intent. You may go now if you choose. But they will be sure to call on you later, if you do."

"I have half a mind to make them come and find me," Horus said. After a minor show of defiance, though, he softened. "But now, I suppose there's no sense doing anything out of sheer spite. Where are Demicolon and Pseudofluff now?"

They each gestured with a tentacle. "We will show you where you may wait for them."

At first, Horus was antsy. He tapped claws noisily on the table. He felt slighted, being asked to sit in a side-room and wait on the prosecutors. They arranged for this meeting... why not rather be waiting for *him*? Then it occurred... they *were* Meduselda, and so not very speedy. It was entirely possible the only reason he'd been headed-off and asked to wait was because he'd simply walked out of the courtroom much faster than they could hope to float...

...Their arrival – not long delayed after all – seemed to confirm this...

"Ah, Mr. Templar... well-met!" Demicolon greeted him as he coasted through the doorway.

Pseudofluff, of course, was right behind. "We appreciate you taking time out of your busy schedule to indulge this unexpected council."

Horus stood up. "Mr. Demicolon, Mr. Pseudofluff," he nodded at each. "My schedule is indeed restrictive; I hope you will be brief. But first of all, perhaps you'd better explain the nature of this meeting. Even in your native law, surely the private collusion of both defense and prosecution is... *questionable*, at best."

"No need to mince your words, Counselor," Demicolon said. "Here we may be frank. We have learned a very great deal about you in short order, Horus Templar. And now – no doubt – you have learned something of us, and our intentions."

Horus nodded with narrow eyes. "I've learned that the two of you would force good postmen to betray their principles – and carelessly upend the life of an innocent Clerk – only to further pervert justice by taking our region's highest court and turning it into a lame prop for your Queens' vanity."

"And what of your own vanity, Templar?" Pseudofluff challenged. "You've done well to hide your family's checkered history, but it is not beyond unearthing. We know of your close affiliations with certain – shall we say – extremist groups? Your uncle... your own father..."

Horus stood silently, only just able to contain his alarm and humiliation.

"...We see that even now you go to special pains to bury that unfortunate past," Demicolon went on. "Your attempts to gain liberties for your client for the remainder of his incarceration are also known to us."

This too was a shock. Only Horus himself knew of this... and the one other person who'd laid eyes on the forms...

He shot a look at Jether.

"What?" Jether protested. "Okay, so I chickened out when you sent me to ask them for their list of witnesses! That doesn't mean they didn't ask me a few harmless questions about what *you* were up to."

"Perhaps your definition of harmless and mine don't match up as well as I thought," Horus replied. "We'll discuss it later." He turned back to the prosecutors, looking no less cross. "So you've done some checking up on me. You've discovered I am highly motivated to help my client. Is that so extraordinary for a Public Defender? I'm in no mood to be cleverly cross-examined right now. What is it you want from me?"

"A plea deal," Pseudofluff answered. "Is that so extraordinary for a pair of prosecutors?"

Horus took a moment, rolling his fingers under his chin thoughtfully. He *did* want the lightest sentence possible for Mo. Getting him off entirely seemed already impossible. The facts of the case were too plain and simple: He'd received draft orders that he hadn't followed. One way or another, that was going to come up against him. If the prosecutors were willing to come to the table now, Horus knew he'd better pounce on it, before they realized just how powerless he really was...

...Even so, he would have to feel things out first...

"I'm not sure I understand," Horus admitted. "What does his admission of guilt buy either of you? I don't believe you give a red cent about having my client in your armies. This is about one thing for you: deciding whose Queen is *the* Queen."

"So you have already demonstrated," Demicolon affirmed. "We are not here to buy out your client. We are here to buy *you*. Your cooperation in this endeavor, I mean. Or, at the very least, your non-interference."

"You are a clever one, Templar," Pseudofluff commended him. "But so far your cleverness has only helped to expedite our purposes. Why should that change now? We do not ask much. In fact, we only ask that you do *nothing*. No antics or filibusters... no last-minute monkey-wrenches... none of the sorts ilk you clever Defenders are well-known for. Let us enact the remainder of our plans unchallenged. Forgo any case you might contrive to make. Convince your client to plead guilty."

More and more, Horus didn't like the sound of this. It began to feel too much like making a pact with Wxldlr. But what else could he do for his client?

"What precisely is the scope of your plans?" he boldly asked. "I should like to know that before I agree to anything."

The Meduseldan attorneys gauged each other's blinking luminescence, then returned their focus to him. "We mean to force the Viziers to rule in favor of the one *true* Queen, as you already know," Pseudofluff explained.

"But of course, one of us will feel that the Viziers have chosen erroneously," Demicolon qualified.

"And it is just as well. Asiri would be greatly pleased, if the Tribunal were to rule in her favor. But far from satisfied."

"Nor would Irisa be sated, if she received their award."

"The facts of the matter are simple, Templar," Pseudofluff claimed. "The Annex Tribunal is a very prestigious court, but it is not *the highest* court. And, until all possible rule and authority acknowledges the sole Queenship of Asiri, my work remains unfinished."

"Indeed," Demicolon agreed, at least in part. "The declaration of *Irisa* as rightful inheritor of Berlie Beireldom must come from the very uttermost."

Horus mused. "You both aim for a ruling from the Supreme Ennead? The consensus of all the Viziers throughout the world?"

"We do," Demicolon answered.

"It is simplicity itself," Pseudofluff boasted. "Whichever of us is not awarded by the Tribunal must logically appeal to the Ennead anyway. So long as the Tribunal is forced to rule in favor of one Queen over the other, we will have the necessary grounds to appeal the ruling."

"Our audience before the Ennead will be assured, absolutely."

"And like the Tribunal itself, they will have no choice but to give priority to one Queen – one true heir."

"Favor will have to be bestowed at the highest level... if only we can assure it is bestowed *here*."

"Interesting," Horus said, searching the middle-ground. "But I see a few potential problems for you. Firstly, the Inquisition. The Ennead upholding one of your Queens is no guarantee that the Grand Inquisitors will do likewise. They may be inclined to keep their own council on the matter. I'll admit, you've certainly pulled one over on the courts... but I'd like to see you try and twist the arms of the world's elder-dragons."

"Pish-posh!" Demicolon protested. "When have the Grand Inquisitors and the Supreme Ennead ever been at odds in the past? If anything, they will be grateful that the Viziers have made the choice they themselves have thus far failed to make."

"Fair enough," Horus granted. "But there's still the other problem. The problem of *reaching* the Ennead itself. You will remember: There's been no contact with the Continent for nearly the last half-century. What's your plan to get around that?"

"It is no concern of ours," Pseudofluff waved a dismissive tentacle. "Leave that to the couriers who must deliver the appeal. Leave that to the upstart Rutherford, and his stubborn Post."

Horus found this point especially alarming. Up to now, he could tell himself that what Demicolon and Pseudofluff conspired to do was, in a warped and sinister way, responsible. One Queen of the Berlie Beirels might ultimately *have to be* upheld over the other, lest the whole Dominion be caught-up forever in Civil War. But their ends didn't seem to justify the means. Already, the Post had suffered greatly at their hands. But thinking of the poor postman who might have to go on a suicide mission, simply to deliver that dratted appeal to the Ennead...

"I don't like it," he finally admitted. "It's too callous. We don't know what we'd be sending some unfortunate mail-carrier into..."

"Immaterial," Pseudofluff argued. "It is their duty. Why consider the plight of an anonymous postman, when you should be thinking about your client? That is *your* duty. We can make his sentence quite light, you know."

He forced the question. "How light?"

"We would agree to require Mobipetrolluck to serve only one death in the military," Demicolon answered. "After which, he would be welcome to return to Clerk duties in your Jast-Madiir."

"He will certainly have paid his dues," Pseudofluff agreed. "He will have already served a much higher purpose."

Horus agonized. It was a *very* good deal, well argued...

"Think of it, Mr. Templar," Demicolon continued, as if Horus needed them to push any harder. "Think of the amnesty your action will inspire here, were we to share word of it. The heir of terrorists, extending the olive branch to those who wronged his ancestors. You would help not one Berlie Beirel only, but *all* Berlie Beirels."

Horus deliberated so intensely, his face felt ready to bust. Until finally, he knew there was only one answer he could give in the moment...

"I'll have to consider it," he said.

"You may," Demicolon allowed. "Only don't take too long."

"You heard the Viziers," Horus replied. "The floor is yours tomorrow, regardless. I'll have my decision by the next court day."

"Very good," Pseudofluff bobbed his approval. "Until then, Mr. Templar."

"Good day," Horus dismissed them. And then, like a pair of phantasms, they flew silently from the room...

"What's the matter, Mr. Templar?" Jether asked earnestly. "Doesn't all this intrigue charge you up? You look kinda drained."

"More than a little," Horus said. He let out a long, labored sigh. "It's been a long, *long* day. And I can't help feeling I've just hired out to be a hatchet-man..."

Chapter 11

From the very first watch, the nightmares were relentless. Truly exhausted, Horus had turned in early, hoping to find some quality sleep hidden in the vast abundance of hours he set aside for it. But by the early second watch – about 0:23 – he decided it was useless. He got up, took a small dinner he'd planned to skip, and promptly got back to deliberating the question: Should he or shouldn't he take Demicolon and Pseudofluff up on their deal?

He tried the logical approach to the question again: How could he hope to obstruct them anyway? The Viziers had already conceded to let arguments be introduced as to which Queen was the Queenliest. Was it even possible to wrest the focus of the case away from that impossible question, now that it was broached? For the life of him, he couldn't see how. Just trying to conceive a way proved time and again to be a fast-track to nowhere. He'd always come up completely blank, his fur would crawl with frustration, and he'd ultimately find himself grousing over his great fatigue, marveling at its many indicators. His hands were unsteady. The skin under his eyes sagged, such that he could see the insides of his lower lids. His palate was parched and dry, and turning a surprisingly repugnant sort of rancid. And so the list would go on and on, until finally it would dawn on him that his thoughts had wandered into a useless rut again...

At which point, he would return to the moral approach: How critical was it to resist Demicolon and Pseudofluff? Could his reluctance to capitulate to their scheme be misplaced? Sooner or later, he would always return to the plight of the messenger who would be expected to cross the ocean – to deliver the inevitable appeal to the Supreme Ennead. He tried excusing it, reminding himself that he'd once gladly sent one of his own clients on a seemingly doomed expedition to the mainland, and even been honored to do it. Would sending a duty-bound postman be any different? But, of course, he knew right away that it would. He'd bought his client Rythigaar a chance at a new life – however distant and uncertain – when his old life proved truly forfeit. But in this case, it would be very much the opposite. Any noble and devout postman who volunteered for the mission – or worse, was chosen for it – would be surrendering the life he currently had. And how would the Post respond to such a charge, if they could never be sure afterward that the message reached its destination? Would they send messenger after messenger? Would Horus be endorsing the possible doom of not one, but a whole *series* of Post officers? Would he pen his own intended message of goodwill between Mesomelae and Berlie Beirels in the complex proteins of innocent Phage? But on the other hand, how accountable was he? The appeal was almost certainly unavoidable. And in all the region's past affiliations with the Continent, did he honestly believe the Post was not already being entrusted with these kinds of dubious expeditions all the time? It seemed to come down to some equation of how much blame he was willing to share, and what level of amnesty it might actually inspire if he did. But he couldn't balance either variable, much less both of them...

He sighed away the whole thing, checking the time. Just after 5:00. Most everything would still be closed. But he *could* get into the local Dronehood office, and check up on some of the permission slips he'd filled out for Mo. At the rate they consumed paperwork, no doubt it was processed by now. Perhaps afterward he could endeavor to find something cheap and edible at an all-hours diner, and then go check on the rest of the slips he'd turned in to the justice department the day before. He hoped those would also be processed. He'd promised to meet his client before court today, and it would certainly be preferrable to do it with all arrangements already made...

His early-morning errands were an unqualified success. All permissions attained, a bit of breakfast in him, and hyped-up by the invigorating effects of a bracingly cold stroll back and forth across town, Horus made his way for the Tribunal with a much-needed pep in his step. And as he went, he found his thoughts resting pleasantly on his extremely brief meeting with his secretary the day before. Though it had been enervating in the moment, he remembered that she had promised to attempt a proper visit sometime today. Well he knew, he needed it. He needed her help deciding on his course of action in the coming days of the trial. He needed her insight... her wisdom... her perspective. He needed her.

...Horus made a face to himself as he walked briskly. Perhaps, even in the privacy of his thoughts, it was better to merely admit that he *would value* her input...

* * *

"Good morning, Mo," Horus said, watching his client be brought to him as he stood in a reception room outside of the detention block.

"Allo, Mr. Templar," Mo called back. "Mighty fine to see you, it is! Seems to be my day for the unexpected."

"Well, don't forget, I promised to come see you this morning. To answer your questions."

"Well, blimey if I ain't plum forgot what questions I 'ad before!" Mo replied, alight with confustication. "Sure enough, you said you'd come an' see me... that much I remember plain. But one thing drives out another, an' I've 'ad at least one puzzler too many. They tell me my lawyer's 'ere to see me, an' I think to meself, 'Eh, good on 'im! 'E's probably just round the bend!' Only they don't bring you 'round, no Sir! They open the cell an' bring me out to *you*! Not only that... they go an' remove me shackles! I ain't been out o' them yet, Sir... not once since my arrest. But 'ere I am – a known crook – floatin' about unfettered in the lobby, talkin' with you! 'Ow do you account for that, Mr. Templar?"

Horus grinned. "Well, you see, Mo, today's questions and yesterday's are one and the same. This is about those permissions I was arranging for you." He reached into his jacket and grabbed a certificate, handing it off to Mo. "You've been granted a work release! As a non-violent criminal, you made an excellent candidate. All it took was a few forms!"

Mo unfolded the papers, studying them while Horus looked on. He fully expected his client to burst into some joyous exclamation or other straight-off. But a silent second went by, and another... and it didn't take Horus long to feel any Clerk should've absorbed the substance by now...

"You do understand, don't you, Mo? I've already cleared it with the local Dronehood office! You'll be granted a continuance of your work until sentencing is passed down. You're a Clerk again!"

"Crikey, Mr. Templar... I don't know what to say," Mo admitted at length, not sounding joyous at all.

Horus' brows drew together. "But surely, you're pleased? You have your life back... if only for the time being. That must mean something to you."

"Oh, it does, Sir... that it does, truly!" He still failed to sound better than half-hearted. "Only... I wonder. I wonder if I really ought to 'ave things go so good."

Horus' teeth ground a little in his clenching jaw. He couldn't understand where this was going. And he couldn't understand why he couldn't understand. "What do you mean?"

"Blast if this isn't a pickle," Mo lamented. "But you must understand, Mr. Templar... I've 'ad a peck of time t' think on me crimes. Those attorneys in there, they spoke right enough: One Queen or the other was owed me service, if not both. Only I didn't answer the call! It's not that I don't want t' get me old life back... far from it, Sir. But 'oldin' onto it, when I needed t' let go... well... look at all it's caused! And it gets me wonderin'... it makes me think, Sir... maybe I really *ought* to be locked up for a while. Do me time. Pay the penalty. I just don't want t' pretend like it's nothin', Sir... what I've done. Not anymore."

Horus stroked his muzzle, shook his head. "You're going to pass up your work release?"

Mo sighed. "It pains me to do it, Sir... 'specially knowin' the trouble you must've gone to. Most unexpected of all, this is. But I just don't 'ave the 'eart for it. The old joys be'ind the counter would only be a reproach now. I 'ope you understand, Sir."

Horus' understanding was unfortunately nowhere to be found. All he felt in the moment was frustration... a powerful resentment for making a good gesture, and being shot down by some overreaching attack of conscience from deep in left field. This was presently all he had to give to his client... the one assured concession in his entire arsenal... the best olive branch he could extend to Berlie Beireldom within his own means and clear moral parameters. And it had been rejected. Unforeseeably, flatly rejected...

"Very well," he managed, hardly daring to breathe, for what anger might slip out. "You are at liberty to reconsider any time during the remainder of the trial. I strongly advise that you do." He nodded the best diplomatic nod he could. "Good day, Mo." He turned to *go*...

"Does that mean I won't see you at the trial today, Sir?" Mo called after him. "Am I to be excluded?"

Horus stopped despite himself. "No," he explained over his shoulder. "You'll see me there. But don't expect to hear much from me. It's been arranged: Today belongs to the prosecutors."

* * *

As planned, Demicolon and Pseudofluff did indeed take firm custody of the session that followed. The Tribunal chamber was filled to overflowing with paired torrents of deposition on behalf of Asiri and Irisa, each striving mightily to drown the other out. Occasionally – if only for the novelty – Horus actually tried to focus on the arguments of one prosecutor or other. But no matter how he exerted himself, it was impossible to catch more than a few words in a row out of the overall racket. A crossfire of loud and zealous words rebounded off the walls, forcing the attorneys to compete with their own arguments, as well as each other's. The constant buffeting of the two voices combined with total exhaustion kept Horus blinking hard and shaking himself just to stop his eyes from crossing. And even when he did, on occasion, manage to tune them out enough to allow for a bit of actual thought to take place, he found no real relief. Even in his own mind, all was sound and fury, signifying nothing. His gaze occasionally wandering to Mo, he dratted his fruitless generosity. Blankly watching the babbling attorneys, he dratted the horrible decision looming just ahead of him. And watching his aide – the boy-wonder, perched where there ought to be a secretary – nod-off, he dratted his loneliness... his unfair feelings of forsakenness. Through it all, he could see no way forward. He'd never been so down and out. He presently lacked the strength to muster even a single positive thought. And, for the duration of that interminable shouting match, he resigned from even trying...

"Order, order!" Vizier Arcturus called over the impassioned spiels of the prosecutors. The words shook Horus from a virtual stupor. After a brief glimpse at the thoroughly shell-shocked looking court recorder, he checked the time and saw that – scarcely an eternity later – they'd actually arrived at 16:00... the end of the court day...

"We shall have order!" Arcturus persisted, until at last the drones faded to a halt. "The time we have set for your arguments has elapsed."

"But your Honors," Pseudofluff appealed, "we have hardly begun to..."

"It is *elapsed,*" Arcturus explained more thoroughly. "Do the prosecutions have any remaining case to present which does *not* pertain directly to this matter of right of succession?"

They checked with one another. "No, your Honor," Demicolon answered. "If we are not permitted to further expound on this point, then the prosecutions rest."

"Good," Arcturus sighed. "Then we shall duly move forward. The defense will present its own case in two days."

This surprised everyone, including Horus. *"Two* days, your Honor?" Pseudofluff inquired. "We are to have an extra day of recess?"

"Yes," Arcturus answered, before digging a fist into the top of his head. "Creators know, we could use it."

* * *

"So, I think I might've slept through most of Demicolon and Pseudofluff's filibusters," Jether admitted later, once again attending to the countless books he'd ordered after they'd returned to Horus' bungalow. "Could you give me the highlights? What did I miss?"

"I'm afraid I haven't the foggiest," Horus replied. "And I was awake for it all." He cradled his head as he stared an empty stare. "*Every word.*"

"Have you decided what you're going to do about their deal?" Jether pressed him as he put another book on the shelf.

"No," Horus sighed. "But at least I have another day to think about it."

"Really, Mr. Templar, just take them up on it. It's *so* simple! It fits with all your objectives."

Horus checked his timepiece again. His hope of seeing Deborah today was nearly gone. As if a single day could know any more disappointment...

"I'm thinking about it, Jether. But a deal like this has broad implications. You heard how the Post would be unduly involved in the scheme... and not for the first time. I don't wonder if I should go and talk to them myself... see how they feel about carrying such a message..."

"Rutherford himself said they'd still deliver mail for those guys," Jether reminded him. "That feels like permission to me. Think about the time that would mean! A trip that long would take weeks... maybe months. More likely than not, we'd never get word back from the Ennead *at all*. Mo might just get to live out the rest of his days as a Clerk... just as if you'd actually won the case."

"That might be all well and good," Horus said, looking back at him, "...except that Mo doesn't wish to exercise his work release."

Jether paused mid-book-placing. "He doesn't?"

"No."

"Why in the world not?"

Horus shook his head. "I'm not entirely sure. He attempted to convey some question of conscience."

The boy blinked. "Man, your client's even weirder than you."

Horus watched yet another book go up... out of numeric order. He'd told Jether his preference to have them sequential at least a half-dozen times already. The boy always had some airy excuse... "okay," "sure," "yeah," he would say... then go right back to his stupid Dudley Decimal System. It made Horus seethe inside... forced him to look for some diversion from his frustration. He reflexively checked his watch again, only to feel his distress compound. "Blast it, Jether... I *told* you those volumes are numbered!" he finally burst. "Put them up that way, or for goodness sake, don't bother to put them up at all!"

Jether froze for a moment, rather astonished. "Geez, Mr. Templar..." he said at length, "...it's about time! I was beginning to think you'd never put your foot down on this."

Horus took a few breaths, made a face. "What do you mean?"

"It was a test, Sir," he explained. "A manufactured incident to see how long it would take you to actually stop me doing something the wrong way. And I'm sorry to say, you blew it. My folks would have exploded right from the beginning! That's what any mentor worth his salt would do."

Horus turned back to the fore, shut his eyes hard. "I think I'd rather be having nightmares of empty chairs right now," he said.

"You do seem even dumpier than usual, if you don't mind my saying so, Mr. Templar," Jether pitied him. "Really long in the face. Either you're way older than I even guessed, or you haven't been sleeping well. Maybe what you need is a good sedative. Why not see my aunt? I'm sure she could help."

"*Your aunt*," Horus almost chuckled. "About the *last* person I would want to see," he admitted without a thought. But then, realization struck him hard. "Good gracious," he breathed. "But I should be visiting Milo! It may be my last chance to see him before the operation..."

He checked his watch yet again. For the umpteenth time, he was torn... torn between staying – clinging to the shadow of a hope that Deborah might still show – or going to make what could very well be his final visit to a friend not long for this world...

"You should go, Mr. Templar," Jether said knowingly. "She would've been here by now if she was coming. You ought to accept that."

Horus hesitated another moment. Then, drawing a resolute breath, he collected himself and stood up. "I fear you're right. Too much these days, I've wondered what I'll be called on to accept..."

* * *

The road to Dr. Nokkaeru was an appropriately dark one. The twilight proved even more frigid than the morning, a somber wind moaning down into the cold stone trenches. By the time he reached the outpatient facility, Horus was thoroughly harried. He had to push the door shut behind him before quickly wrapping his coat tight one last time. Naturally, the Herons in the reception room all looked at him unsympathetically. But once he'd called on the desk, he couldn't complain about the service. No sooner than he asked to see Dr. Nokkaeru, and they brought him back to her office, straight away...

He had but to enter the room and feel he'd made a gross semantic error. He'd expected to see Deputy Constable Miloje put up in there, but the man was nowhere to be found. He darned himself for asking after the physician rather than the patient. But oddly, upon further examination he found that the Doctor was out, as well. Horus had to scratch his head at that. He wasn't sure why the staff would bring him back to her empty office. But before he could backtrack and begin to sort things out, Nokkaeru arrived, let herself in...

"Ah, Counselor Templar," she said, far too pleased to see him. "My thanks for making a call; I regret that I have not checked up on you myself. Tell me, how is Jether? Has he been thoroughly infuriating?"

"Very much so, yes," Horus nodded.

"Wonderful," Nokkaeru replied, stepping into a basin before putting on fresh leather gloves. "You are yet under considerable strain... that is plain to see. I am rather surprised you would seek my help, but of course, it is gladly offered." She snatched up an inflatable bag attached to a pressure gauge. "Roll up your sleeve now, would you?"

Horus threw up defensive hands. "I think you mistake my reasons for coming," he said. "I'm not here for a checkup; I wanted to look in on Miloje. I thought, perhaps, a little company before the procedure..."

"Thoughtful, Counselor, but untimely," she began to explain. "I fear your presence will be no comfort now. He has passed beyond my care."

For some reason, she paused at this juncture. Horus felt his gut drop like a rock. "He... you mean, he's...?"

"Oh, dear, no," she nearly laughed. "He is not *dead*, if that is your mind. Rather, he has been interned for final testing. If all goes well, he will be ruled fit for surgery, and we will begin implantation at once. But this process shall be rigorous; you won't be able to see him or learn of his fitness for a few days." Her look remained intent. "In the meantime, I see no reason why I cannot provide you with some obviously needed medical consultation." She gestured to a strangely-placed couch. "Have a seat, Counselor."

Horus hesitated, but eventually obliged, privately beginning to warm-up to the idea of that sedative Jether had mentioned. "This is rather unnecessary," he argued anyway, even as he sat down. "I'm in good health, apart from a minor case of sleep deprivation."

"Balderdash," she contended. "You are a walking derelict. Though, I suspect your issues are primarily psychological. Even so, I stand capable of rendering expert care."

Horus winced. "You? A psychiatrist? But didn't you yourself tell me only a few months ago that you had no such training?"

She held her head up proudly. "I have since familiarized myself with the basic tenets. And why not? After all, I have observed that the mind is far and away the most widely defective constituent."

"I see," Horus replied skeptically. "And what are some of these basic tenets of psychiatry?"

"Firstly, a couch is required. Hence the furnishings in which you presently find yourself situated. But you must recline. Even to sit may unduly inhibit the treatment of your psyche." She came up to him, holding a talon out. "I will also need you to pay in advance. Five shillings, if you please."

"Five shillings?" he asked. "I'm a little hard-up right now... are you sure you couldn't bill me later?"

"I most certainly cannot! This is another of the basic tenets which must be observed. Now stop your bellyaching, or I will make it seven shillings." She momentarily curled her clawed fingers in a 'fork it over' gesture.

Horus sighed, then reached for his moneybag...

* * *

"Things have been rather difficult lately," he admitted, laid out on the couch, facing away from the Doctor, as he watched his thumbs twiddle.

"You mentioned trouble sleeping, I believe," she coached him. Her voice sounded impassive and professional, though he knew deep-down she was relishing every moment of examining his miseries.

"Yes," he replied. "On account of a recurring nightmare – a twisted memory of my previous case. I go to look at my client, but he isn't there. It's just an empty chair next to me. True enough... that's how it really went. It was one of those dreadful *In Absentia* cases. But in the dream, I expect him to be there. He's *supposed* to be. But there's never a man in the chair."

"Interesting," she mused. "In the dream, you are supposed to be representing a man... but in fact, you are representing no man." She paused, struck by her own words. "It does sound strangely ominous, put just that way." She waved it off. "But never mind. How do you think this subconscious fixation is significant?"

"I've wondered that very thing for weeks," he sighed. "I wish I had an answer I thought I could work with. I know I have a tendency to take my defeats rather hard..."

"You do have an unhealthy concern for the welfare of others, I have always found," she commented.

"...*In Absentia* defeats are especially hard to stomach," he went on, ignoring her. "But this one tops them all. I can't seem to shake it."

"Do you suppose there are other stressors which would tend to magnify your unrest?"

"Certainly, there are," Horus replied. "No matter how I try, all my interactions with my client have been train wrecks. The case itself has been a barrage of legal and ethical dilemmas, all impossibly muddled up. Then, of course, there's your nephew."

"Yes," she nodded knowingly.

"As for the rest of my ills, well..." he hesitated. "You were there. You saw what happened." He tried to sound nonchalant, even as he avoided specifics.

"*I did,*" she agreed, suddenly sounding more intent. "And now, I think, we come to the real core of the matter... the new relevance of the empty chair..."

Horus' heart leapt. He searched for a dismissive response, even as he worked to untie the knots in his throat. "You'll forgive me if I doubt that very much," he managed.

"And where you should not," she cautioned. "You must consider that the subconscious has essentially boundless powers of metaphor. That is perhaps *the most* foundational precept of psychiatry. The empty chair has evolved its meaning, Counselor. It no longer represents your past failure... but rather, your present feelings of abandonment." Her enthusiasm grew notably as she expounded. "Hear now the unvarnished truth: Secretary Boulevard's absence wounds you. You feel a critical piece of yourself has been torn away. It haunts you in the waking hours and terrorizes you at night. You are loath to admit it, but you've truly forgotten how to function without her. It's been all you can do to hold back the river, and now it is about to burst! You cannot bear to be kept apart!"

"And that's not even the worst of it... is it?" Horus replied. His voice was not pained, nor reserved, nor fearful. He wasn't crying buckets, as she likely hoped he would. It was an earnest question. This proved enough to throw Dr. Nokkaeru for a loop...

"What did you say?" she asked at length.

He sat up, searching her with one of those courtroom gazes... the kind meant to ferret-out the truth and draw it to the surface with all necessary force. "You failed to mention the most horrific part," he explained again. "The real agony isn't in being kept apart now. It's being cursed with every confidence that she's gone *forever.*"

Nokkaeru marveled somewhat at this. "You admit it openly."

"And why shouldn't I?" Horus asked, continuing to ply his craft. "It's clear to me now... you knew about this all along." He stood. "You once told me there was great and sudden disaster looming in my future. You couldn't help yourself, letting me know how eager you were to see it." He gestured around the room. "And now, here we are. Congratulations. I hope it's everything you imagined." He felt his jowls twisting and quivering as he went on, looking at that cruel woman. "But you don't seem satisfied. What more do you want me to say? You were right. I'm every bit as miserable as you claim. I'm ready to go to pieces. Oh, I know I'll *survive* without her... but I never realized before just how much I don't want to. And now that I do, it's too late." His face ached with tension. He threw up his hands. "You'll forgive me if I have no more words. You're about the last person I would want to confide in. And now you know my deepest secret."

The room was quiet and still. Horus was aware of little besides his strained breathing and the armed unrest of his tear ducts, still fighting to break loose. His eyes may've been foggy, but he didn't oblige the Doctor the sight of a single tear. And as the seconds lengthened on, he actually began to feel a bit better. This certainly wasn't the forum he would've chosen, but for better or worse, he'd finally allowed himself to externalize his pain... and even, in an odd way, feel as if he'd confronted his tormentor. Yes, he took an easier breath... he found that he *did* feel relieved...

...And then, she laughed...

"Oh, Counselor... you are such a card," she said, as she reined-in her mirth. "I concede, it has been most amusing to observe you in your present state of upheaval. But if you *truly* believe this is the moment I once foreboded – your moment of incredible, sublime calamity – then you are doomed to be quite disappointed, and your future even more piteous than I dared suspect!"

As if his emotions could further exert themselves to new extremes, sudden anxiety threatened to overwhelm him. "*How*? How could that possibly be? Don't you understand? Didn't I make it clear enough? I'm about to lose the most important person in my life! I may have lost her already! How can you insist that something *worse* is coming... even *much* worse?"

"You must remember the way I characterized your pending disaster, dear man," she responded, shaking her head at him. She got up from her rather booth-like desk and began to pace the room. "Did I not say that it would transcend the mundane, familial sort of drama? I am certain that I *did*. Your affections for your secretary are quaint, but you might find such fondness in another, given time. You are not as lost as your frazzled emotions make you out."

"Then *tell me* what more I have to lose," he implored, despite himself. This was why he'd tried to draw the truth out of her to start with: a horrible need for confirmation. He had to ***know*** this really was his moment of rock-bottom. And now – having learned it wasn't – there was no solace to be had. He could only mine for more information, and in so doing at least try to brace himself...

His question made her stop. She trained her horrible goggles on him, as if to project the image of a cold and heartless future. "You forget your deeper bedrock – your cornerstone, on which you base your whole understanding of reality. Your virtues, your values – your foundational parameters of right and wrong, and the way you perceive their hierarchy... both within the cosmos, and beyond it. You forget your *beliefs*. You think them so, but they are *not* adamant. I posit they will be shaken, Counselor. Shaken to the core, if not altogether shattered. You will stand high on your platform of justice, only to watch it go to work destroying and displacing. You will seed your good intentions and watch as multitudes reap grief and ruin. And in due course, you will question that which you deem unquestionable. Yes, Horus Templar, even you. One day, you will come face-to-face with what it truly means to be *lost*."

Hearing this, Horus was not at all affected the way he thought. Finally, it seemed, the Doctor had gone too far... overreached almost laughably in her constant efforts to unsettle him. He couldn't so much as consider that what she said was true. It frankly didn't even make sense. Justice was simple, and by very definition equitable... and good was far too powerful to be warped to evil purposes...

"Ridiculous," he dismissed it. "Patently absurd." But even as he spoke the words, a tiny shard of doubt took root.

"Excuse my words as you will," she replied, turning away huffily. "I have told you your future as best I can attempt to discern it. But I have never presumed to be a proper prognosticator. The ability to see anything clearly is far beyond my scope. Indeed, I lack the power even to predict whether you will receive your beloved secretary back from the man Snozzwell or not."

"Where would I have to go?" Horus asked. Again, it seemed, his forthright question surprised her. "Who could I see about it? Surely someone in this country could tell me." He sat back on the couch, eyes scanning the floor. "I just can't handle the uncertainty anymore. Even knowing we'd never work together again would be better. At least then, I could stop worrying and begin to move on."

She pondered a spell. "It is a hard question. Such comprehensive foresight as you seek is exceptionally rare... and few who possess it would dare make it known." She tapped her talon under the jagged beak of her mask. Until finally, something must've clicked. "But there is the rumor..."

Horus huffed, in too deep to bother backing out now. "What rumor?"

"It has been suggested the Proconsul himself may visit the tradeshow this year," she answered, prompting his own memory of the suggestion. "*His* gifts are the stuff of legend... and much fearful hearsay, besides." He could swear he saw her shudder...

For his own part, Horus became aware of some apprehension. "Zedulon's prophetic powers are certainly renowned. He's understood to be nearly unrivaled, even among Proconsuls."

"That man is no mere Proconsul," she pronounced, almost involuntarily. "I have been in his presence before; I have felt the terrible onus that rests on him. I tell you: It's like is not to be found... and well, I deem, he knows it. He is secretive and reclusive, even by our standards. He keeps his own council. As sovereigns go, he is not fondly loved... but he *is* feared, which of course is greater still. I can reveal little more, except that there is surely due cause for it." She gave Horus another quick study. "Come to think of it, there are some uncanny similarities between his tragic aspect and yours. It might be very interesting to arrange for the two of you to meet."

"Is such a meeting possible?" he asked. "Could you arrange it?"

"Hmm," she answered. "We are assuming he shows at all. You must remember it is only a rumor."

"Supposing he does."

She nodded at length. "As a Plague Doctor of some distinction, I believe I could. It is possible."

Horus curled his whiskers. He strained to resolve on a course of action. "It's a remarkable prospect. A bit overwhelming to think about. Now it comes to it... I'm not sure. I seem to be unsure of a lot of things, these past few days."

"There is no cause for haste," she reminded him. "Whether he comes or nay, he is not *here*. You can avail yourself of time to think about it."

Horus sighed, got back up. "Just what I need... another thing to think about." He pulled his jacket tight around him, remembering the chilling wind-tunnels he was about to brave. "Give my regards to the Deputy Constable, if you have occasion," he said solemnly as he made for the door.

She nodded. "I will."

Chapter 12

Art sat across the room from her, his eyes gliding slowly back and forth along the wide brim of her hat, evidently in search of something... he knew not what. Occasionally, he'd stray up to her ears poking through the top, or down to the outline of her snout, facing away. And all the while, he wondered. Any other time, he would've been unreservedly happy to share a moment of respite like this with her, sitting together in a finely furnished room, watching her fix a peaceful gaze on the fireplace. But right now, he was only... well, *puzzled*. He couldn't seem to put his finger on it, but something felt vaguely screwy...

Growing restless, he moved over to a nearby window, through which light *poured* into the room... with generosity and to spare. He looked out the pane, quickly finding the outside world held no more answers than that fondly familiar hat. Mostly, he just found just more of that blinding *light*. He tried to pick out some feature of the world beyond... tried to focus on anything at all. But he quickly tired of the attempt. And soon, all memory of even trying passed on. Taking a cold sip from his metal cup, he just stared out into nothing particular, appropriately blank...

"When did I get back?" he asked at some point. He seemed to enjoy ample time to ponder each of the words himself. Had he spoken them at all, or merely thought them? He was unsure, if not overly concerned...

"Two days ago," Blucille answered, just before he might've let the question slip away. *Two days ago*, he repeated to himself, whether aloud or in his head. It seemed to merit some consideration. He wasn't at all sure where he'd been before that. But finally, with some effort, it was coming back to him...

"Yes... I remember now," he said. "It was the Cult job. The Digit Cults."

"The doctors said you'd be delirious for a while," she explained, only after another long pause. It wasn't distinct, but Art could almost swear his sharp ears caught some distant whispering in the sonic void between her responses. No matter, of course... probably just someone in the other room. Perhaps the doctors. It was always so easy to explain away...

"Right," he went along. "They were messing with my head. Trying to get me to think crazy things." His eyes wandered back into the room. He saw the poker next to the fireplace... considered stirring the coals. It was getting a bit chilly. Or, maybe it'd been chilly all along. But he quickly noticed it was no use. The fireplace was empty anyway.

"Do you remember anything else?" Blucille asked, never so much as flinching. "What did they tell you? What was it they wanted you to think?"

Art deliberated on that point. Of all things, this should've been clear and present – it was a matter of fundamental conviction. But he found himself going back and forth between two diametrically-opposed ideas, honestly fudging which he'd believed all his life, and which they'd been forcing on him. Finally, he just chose what his gut told him...

"They... they wanted me to believe the thumb was never a finger," he worked out. Simply saying it seemed to fill the room with a powerful disappointment. This time, he felt more sure than ever of those whispers, off in the other room...

"No, Dear," Blucille finally lamented. "They wanted you to believe the thumb *was* a finger. They wanted you to believe a horrible lie. But you and I... we know better. We've *always* known better. Haven't we, Dear?"

"*Dear*?" Art repeated. He searched the motionless back of Blucille's head, now more focused, while his vague misgivings blossomed into a powerful doubt. "No..." he protested. "No, something's not right here. You... you're not right." He grabbed his head, wishing it were a bellows he could squeeze the fog out of. "There you are... your voice... your hat... your ears. But your eyes... let me see your eyes, Blucille."

She sat, perfectly still and silent. She would not turn to regard him. Seconds passed. He watched breathless for some sign. *Any* sign. Not a muscle in her whole body twitched...

"You won't look at me," he declared, shaky and dizzy. "Why won't you look at me?!"

"She isn't real, Mallard," a voice informed him. It was *clear*... the one clear thing in all this uncanny business. And so present. He *knew* the voice... knew it with the same familiarity as his own thoughts. He strove and struggled to assign a name to the voice. Then, he heard the door open behind him...

"*Sabracore*," he said.

"Yes," the Bishop sighed. "Here we find ourselves again, you and I... still working to get past this one simple point. I've got to hand it to you... you're even more stubborn than I thought. Truly one of my most resilient subjects. I really thought I'd have you with this one. But you just keep *holding out*."

Art watched as the charade began to unravel before his eyes. 'Blucille' was nothing more than a prop... a dummy's head – and not even a very lifelike one – set up in a high-backed chair with a hat over it. The blinding light in the windows was just that – the impression of the outside world, a paper-thin façade. The room itself, a superficial redressing of the Sanctum...

"...And it really is too bad," Sabracore went on, lamenting. "You should've responded to a little encouragement from a friendly persona. If you had, I might've let you keep her." He reached ominously for a chain in his pocket. "But now, it looks as though I'll have to take her away from you..."

"Wait," Art implored him... half-begging, half trying to sort it all out. "What about her voice? It was *her* voice coming from the dummy! How did you do that?!" A horrible thought struck him. He glared at the Bishop. "You... you got to her? Just to get to *me*!? Show me where she is! If you harmed so much as a hair on her, I swear I'll..."

"No, Dear," Blucille's voice cut him off. "You and I, we know better," it continued in mock fashion. "We've always known better." Art turned back to the doorway, smelling someone come in. "Haven't we, Dear?" It was Teresa standing there, speaking Blucille's words. He looked into her eyes, feeling freshly betrayed. She soon averted his look.

"I..." Art stammered, "...But *she*... she sounds just like *her*..."

"So we've convinced you," Sabracore explained, flashing with amusement. "You don't remember what your district attorney friend *really* sounds like anymore. Teresa's voice was... an expedient replacement."

"No way!" Art swore. "I could *never* forget what she sounds like! Not in a million years!"

"You already have," Sabracore informed him calmly. "And now, for your impudence, I'll have to make you forget a whole lot more..."

He drew his watch. Art was sent careening once again in the imaginary vortex of swirling, subliminal essence...

"We're paring down the voices in your head, Mallard," the Bishop's augmented voice declared through the chaos. "Soon the only one left will be mine."

Art rallied all his strength and willpower in a last-ditch effort to shield his eyes. "I'll fight you to the very end," he said weakly. "I'm still in this thing."

"For the moment. But you're slipping. You have no idea how close you are to *cracking*. You want my advice? Let it go. It's the full light of day waiting for you, just on the other side of that thick skull of yours."

He squinted, never quite able to close his lids. "I'm... I'm not buying it, Sabracore. Nothing true could come of all this hookey-pook and misdirection you're into."

"That's a conceit. Truth takes more work than anything. It's lies that come easy." He sighed, quickly growing weary of Art's resistance. "I can see we have our work cut out for us today..."

He drew a second watch. Mallard was overwhelmed at once...

* * *

When he came back to himself, Art was unsurprised to find he'd been returned to his cell. It was a long, treacherous climb back to proper consciousness. He hoped his throbbing head and exhaustion meant he hadn't slept away too much time. But the more he considered it, a short sleep was really no comfort. Sabracore could've plied his dark mindcraft for any length of time before that... even *days*...

Days. A rogue thought struck him. *Friday*...

Was it even possible he hadn't already missed it? How much had the world passed him by, down in that timeless dungeon? Were the cops even looking for him yet? Had they already given up?

Supposing they *were* looking for him right now. He despaired for some way to leave them a clue... a trail of breadcrumbs. He really *was* cracking. Any hope of that sort of thing was long lost. He had no way of retroactively connecting where he had been to where he was now, no matter how bad he wanted to...

But what about escaping? He hadn't even tried to yet... if memory served. There might be some promise there. He had a very distinct feeling that the game was in an advanced stage now. It wasn't just Sabracore's assurances he was about to lose it... he could feel the wear on his mind all too well for himself. Maybe an escape attempt at this late hour would really throw them off... catch them unawares. Or, maybe they'd be one step ahead of him like always, and he'd only be walking into another fiendish illusion...

Art sighed. If he was honest, most of the time he couldn't even be sure which way was up anymore. Next time he saw a policeman... or Blucille... he might not even know them from the real thing...

He pushed the thought away. It was just too horrible. He couldn't let himself worry what his mind might lose hold of – what it may have already lost – if he remained obstinate. He *needed* to come up with a way out of this mess! But it was no use. He felt locked out of his own cleverness... and all the thinking in the world couldn't unstick him. He rolled back over and wished for sleep...

Then he heard footsteps... smelled food...

"Go away," he said over his shoulder, when sound of the steps came to a stop just outside. He *was* hungry, but much too despondent to bother eating. However, the goons did their goony thing and refused to oblige him. They started unbolting the door...

"Didn't you hear me?" Art demanded, turning and sitting up. "I said..."

He shut his trap, seeing who it was. This was no goon bringing him sparse pickings. This was Teresa, delivering a whole steaming plate...

"Hi, Art," she said weakly, able to force little eye contact.

"Teresa," Art replied, still rather shocked.

She walked over to him, holding the plate out. "I brought this for you special," she explained.

Art received it carefully, rather taken aback. This was the first thing that felt like real kindness in as long as he could clearly remember. "Thank you." He regretted that he didn't know what more to say.

For her part, Teresa seemed to feel similarly. She lingered a moment, and then surprised him by sitting next to him on the slab. He angled questioning looks between her and the dinner plate. He didn't particularly want to scarf food with her sitting right there, looking mopey... but to do otherwise would probably be even more rude. Slowly, he started eating. She'd left him little choice...

A while later, after his rate of consumption had ramped up a bit, his brain was in somewhat better shape, passing out of feeding-frenzy mode and absorbing some needed nutrition. At this point, he really began to ponder her continued presence. She just kept sitting there, looking down at the floor. Finally, he felt certain there was something she wanted to say. Only, she couldn't... even given a fair amount of hang-time to choose her words. Art strained to imagine what it was she longed to tell him. 'Sorry for ratting you out'? 'Sorry for impersonating your best gal'? But then, she'd been reprogrammed – the way he was being now. Would Sabracore have left enough room for that kind of remorse? Could there even be another explanation for why she was just chilling out in his dreary little cell with him?

At last, he realized all the pondering was getting him nowhere again. It was time for a more straightforward strategy. If she didn't know how to start spilling the beans, he'd engage her instead. They *had* been friends, if only in an unfortunate espionage-reverse-espionage sort of way. And in spite of all she'd done to him, Art didn't like to see her so low...

So, he set his plate aside. His old mentor had taught him that a problem you couldn't fix with your head could sometimes be solved with just a little heart...

"Hey," he said, swallowing the last of what was in his mouth. "Why so down in the dumps?" Yes, if there was one thing Art Mallard had more of than brains and brawn, it was heart...

"I wish I knew," she replied. "I mean, I *do* know. I feel horrible about... all of *this*. Handing you over to the Bishop. Playing a part in his... his methods. But I know I'm supposed to remember that we're helping you... that it'll be worth it in the end. It's just so hard to watch you struggle." She shook her head, never looking above her feet. "I've seen it so many times now. So many others who fought until they couldn't fight anymore. I've... I've caught myself wanting to see it turn out different... just *once*... if only for the sake of novelty. If only to feel like..." She hesitated. Then she bolted up to go in a huff. "Well, never mind. But for what it's worth, Art, I'm sorry. Truly sorry..."

"It's worth a lot," Art called after her, stopping her in her tracks. "An awful lot, really. But I gotta be honest, Teresa... your goodwill alone, much as I appreciate it, isn't going to hold me up for long. I'm liable to forget it, the next time Sabracore takes out a pocket watch. Don't get me wrong: Sympathy is nice and all. But if this thing hurts you as much as it seems to, well..." he paused a moment, though he knew it was time to climb out on a limb, "...maybe you oughta do something about it."

She looked back at him, her face flushing as her emotions ran high. "What would you have me do!? I can't go against *him*! That part of me is gone. He destroyed it... just the way he always does."

Art shook his head. "I don't believe that. His hold on you isn't unbreakable, Teresa. If it was, you wouldn't be here now. You wouldn't feel *sorry*. You really want to see things turn out different, just once? Why not *be* the different one yourself!"

"I can't. There's no way."

"There *is*." He chuckled. "Oh, sure, I know that's rich coming from me. What've I got to lose, asking you to do something crazy?" He looked at her more serious. "But deep down you know you'd be doing it for more than just me. So I say: Do it. Do it for the ones that'll come after... the ones who'll suffer just as much as we have if you don't. Do it for your own conscience.

You know this is wrong. Even if the thumb's *not* a finger – even if everything Sabracore believes is the truth – this is still no way to serve it."

Teresa was quiet. She was thoughtful. Art held his breath, wondering what way her deliberations would go. When she started for the door again, he despaired, feeling he'd failed utterly at last. But when she got there, she only propped herself up on her toes and looked out the little window, checking the coast was clear. Art's ears perked. He was already pretty sure from the sounds and smells that none of the goons were around, but Sabracore himself had no scent or footsteps, so it was just as well that she made sure...

"Okay," she said... hushed, but resolute. "What do you suggest?"

"Simple," he replied very cool, though inwardly he was ready to happy-dance. "Just walk right into the SAPD and ask for Blucille Cordon. That's my lady friend you were impersonating, if you didn't know."

"I... I don't like the sound of that," she grew reserved again. "Going to the *cops*? It's... it's taking an awful chance, isn't it?"

"Not hardly!" Art laughed it off. "She's a DA... she can cut you a deal for helping save my skin! Besides, you're already on their bad list. They've known you were in the Cult all along!"

"*Great*," she quipped. "But, I guess that does make it a little easier."

Art searched her. "So you'll do it?"

She nodded. "Yeah."

"That-a-girl!" he said, slapping his own knee. "You won't be sorry! I'll make sure of it!"

"Alright," she sighed. This time, she opened the door, leaning back in as she left. "I'm trusting you."

He tipped his head at her. "And I, you. But don't worry: This time I think we can really trust each other."

She grinned weakly. And then, she was gone. The bolt closed loud, seeming to echo far longer than it should have...

Left alone with that hopeless sound still crashing around in his head, Art's last words began to dog him. It could be nothing. Maybe he was right, and he really could trust her now...

...Or maybe this was just another layer of the lie...

Chapter 13

By midday, Horus had quite had his fill of agonizing in a vacuum. The extra day of adjournment proved to be more of a curse than a blessing. Time could certainly be a commodity when making crucial decisions... but left to his own devices, all the time in the world didn't seem to help in this case. Horus would fuss over Demicolon and Pseudofluff's ultimatum until he could stand it no longer... at which point he would always fall back on the question of whether to seek the soothsaying of the Proconsul. And round and round it went...

Until, at last, he remembered something he'd resolved to do earlier... another visit he really ought to make. Once he *finally* had a course of action, he was off to the races. He threw on an extra undershirt and a vest beneath his jacket, grabbed his briefcase and flew right out the door...

The journey proved a long one, with an angry sky rumbling its ominous threats most of the way. Every day he'd spent in Roemnar appeared overcast... until *today*, which made all the prior days seem bright and cheerful by comparison. But even with every warning of an imminent cloudburst, he couldn't seem to sustain his dash. All that initial haste steadily melted under the infectious sulkiness of the heavens, and the questioning looks he got from the other pedestrians in their deliberate, magisterial strides. But while he let the mood of everything rein him back to a shuffle, his conviction to reach his intended destination was undiminished. Come Heck or high water – the onset of the latter seeming all-but inevitable – he would get where he was going...

And so he finally did. Rounding a long, desolate side street, he came to a wider ditch with obvious foreign influence. Here, he found, things were allowed to *grow*. Low shrubs... tiny raft-style bonsai trees... even the dirt and chipped wood they were growing in... Horus had to pause and admire them all. His eyes wandered over both sides of the path he took slowly to the entrance, and all around the building itself, where taller bushes, finely-trimmed, were stationed. The final stretch of the path brought him into a circular garden area at the foot of the stoop, where he found something even more curious... a large monument in the shape of a question mark. He stopped and studied it for a while, wearing an appropriately quizzical expression...

Then at last, he fairly crowded himself up and into the front door – which, while still large enough to accommodate him, felt both too short and too narrow, compared with what he was used to...

"Good morrow, Sir!" a Phage receptionist at a tiny desk greeted him. "If you've come here to send something in the mail, I'm obliged to inform you that this is merely an administrative building," she explained. Then she pointed a spindly little leg. "Nevertheless, there is a collection box up here on your left. We only ask that in the future, you seek out a proper Post Office."

"Thank you very much, and good day," he replied with a nod. "As a matter of fact, I don't have anything to send out. My name is Horus Templar; I'm an attorney here on legal business... though, I confess I don't have an appointment. I wonder if there is any way I could speak with General Rutherford, or one of his lieutenants? Even a staff sergeant would do."

"Mr. Horus Templar, of 17412 Highbrow Street, St. Argonsburg, Jast-Madiir, 41011-0945!" a regal voice beckoned from the doorway, causing Horus to whirl around. "I commend your punctuality, good sir. You've arrived just in time for our meeting."

Horus examined the Postmaster General with relative disbelief. Granted, he'd spent a lot of time lately no better than half-awake, but he felt quite sure he hadn't arranged for this...

"General," Horus acknowledged him, inclining himself. "I would certainly appreciate any time you can spare... that is, if you truly can spare any at all. You're very generous to speak as if we have an appointment to keep. But you and I both know... we don't."

"All evidence to the contrary," Rutherford insisted. "I will be glad to see you in my office presently." He pointed with one leg to a far corner of the room, and the hall beyond. "This way, Mr. Templar."

* * *

Horus felt like a proper giant, wedging himself into General Rutherford's office. Unconsciously, he must've expected something more grandiose – more like a throne room. But the General, majestic though he was, had apparently elected to put himself up in a proper, functional workspace of no obvious distinction... and it showed more and more as Horus attempted to navigate the room. Rather than an elegant chandelier, he merely bumped his head on a simple oak crossbeam. Reaching out to steady himself, he narrowly avoided toppling a bookshelf and filing cabinet, rather than decorative trophies or suits of armor. Yes, these were humble lodgings for a man of Rutherford's station. Horus was glad. At least he had little chance of breaking anything of great value...

Finally, he managed to plop down on the floor in front of Rutherford's desk and begin to feel comfortable. He heard the storm clouds finally begin to unleash their torrent on the outside world, watching water stream down between the blinders. He could almost smell the shrubs out there feasting on the saturated soil. As much as at his first sighting of the Postal Headquarters, he had to marvel at how much he'd missed the simple signs of nature. Then, Rutherford closed the door, and his mind returned at once to the business at hand...

"I do apologize for the limited space," the General said. "If there is anything that might make you more at home, you may request it... though I fear we don't have many of your furnishings to offer."

"It's quite alright, thank you," Horus replied, watching Rutherford round his desk. "I'm only relieved I was able to see you personally, General."

"As am I," Rutherford replied, bringing his disk-like lower body to rest on the floor as well – not quite a 'sit,' per se, but as close as any Phage could do. "You must catch me up on this matter of *Mobipetrolluck vs. the States*. Tell me: How have you faired against those villains, the prosecutors? I hope you have given them what-for. Sorely, I regret I was not able to do more myself to discourage their callous and unscrupulous behavior."

Horus' face drew back. The meeting had only just begun, and already, he started to feel as if he'd let Rutherford down. He cleared his throat. "Yes, well... hardly anything would give me more pleasure than to report they've since been put in their place. But I'm afraid I don't have any such good news. They saw me coming, as much as you... maybe even more so. The whole case has been thoroughly wrangled into a Queen contest. I haven't even managed to impede them."

Rutherford set a pair of his legs on his desk, leaning forward tensely. "But you've devised a gambit, yes? And now you've come seeking my help? Say the word, and it will be granted you! I am given to understand you are a man of high character, Mr. Templar. I am sure you would seek to uphold the virtues of the Post, rather than degrade them, as your opponents have."

Horus' gut just kept plummeting. He was honestly surprised just how much the General had counted on him to ensure Demicolon and Pseudofluff didn't profit in the end from their crooked dealings. Now here he was, come to admit that he was considering colluding with them...

"...Regrettably, I have no such gambit at present," he grudgingly declared. "They both have apparently equal claim on my client – claim that supersedes the citizenship I have to work with. They're holding all the cards." He didn't know where to go from there... except to continue the metaphor. "...Even so, they've offered to deal me in."

Rutherford made no sign, apparently confused. "I... I don't follow, Mr. Templar."

Horus shook his head. "I am sorry, General – I don't mean to be so oblique. Let me come right to the point... Demicolon and Pseudofluff have proposed a plea deal. In exchange for my non-interference, they're willing to ensure Mo receives a light sentence."

The General nodded slowly. "I see. That is, I can appreciate your motives for considering a deal of this sort, in such a pinch. Only... why tell *me*, Counselor? Much as I would like to have seen their conspiracy fail, you are certainly under no obligation to make it happen." He sighed. "And anyway, it is no better than spite for me to seek their downfall now. I fear the worst of their damage is already done."

"It may not be," Horus boded, "which brings us back to the heart of the matter. Our friends the prosecutors seem to have positioned themselves to do you even *more* harm, if I'm not greatly mistaken."

"How so?"

Horus looked down at his interlaced fingers. "Supposing the Viziers were to rule in favor of one Queen. And supposing the injured party was to appeal that decision to the Supreme Ennead. Wouldn't the burden of delivering that appeal fall squarely on the Post's shoulders?"

Rutherford nodded again, more gravely. "Yes. It would be our solemn charge to see their appeal delivered."

"There is no alternative?" Horus pressed. "Carrier pigeons, for instance?"

The General huffed, as if suppressing some distaste at the mere mention of carrier pigeons. "Loath is the Post to employ a mindless creature for such a noble task. But no matter – what you suggest is quite impossible. No bird on the wing could make such an extended journey. It is simply too far."

Horus sighed. "That's just as I feared."

A sympathetic, knowing gleam refracted in the General's spectacle. "I believe I understand now, Mr. Templar. And I appreciate your consideration of our plight. You are indeed most thoughtful."

"Thoughtful, perhaps... for what good all my thinking's done. Answer me honestly, General: Are things with the continent really as bleak as they seem? Surely you would know better than anyone: Has any messenger in the last half-century reached Thaer, and back again? Even one?"

Rutherford shook his head solemnly. "No. Nor do I possess any privileged information as to why. It is a frightful omen."

Horus sat back in dark consideration. "'Frightful' scarcely captures it. And here I held out a bit of foolish hope that something you knew could ease this horrible choice. I can't imagine what's gone wrong between here and Thaer. Nor can I condone sending any postal carrier into the fateful unknown. But at the same time, I don't know what choice I have. If I don't deal, I shan't be able to stop Demicolon and Pseudofluff anyway. I'll simply forfeit what might be my only chance to help a Berlie Beirel – to do my part to bury the hatchet of the 770 Years War."

They sat quiet for a moment while Horus languished in his impasse. But finally, Rutherford managed a low, warm chuckle...

"Don't despair, Horus Templar. Again, I say, it is enough to know your choices are made with conscience. And perhaps I can ease your mind somewhat after all! For it seems you have yet to consider this: An appeal to the Ennead would not be the only correspondence we've been entrusted with delivering to the continent in this time of great severance. You must appreciate the real scope of this thing. Nation has been shorn from nation, son and daughter from mother and father, drone from Dominion. Verily, I would say our burden has been light, all things considered." His faceted head searched a sobering distance, far beyond the walls of his tiny office. "Even so, I have known the blackest burden of command. I have had to send worthy men and women on that path which knows no return. Very soon, we shall have gathered all the mail that we can bear away, and I will have to send another." He turned back to regard Horus. "My people are exceptionally valiant, Mr. Templar, and selfless. I have never hurt for volunteers. But it is a dreadful thing. And yet, there is nothing for it. Duty makes hard demands of us all. No matter how clever we are, we cannot always make things come out as we like. I believe you ought to do what is best for your client – as your duty bids you – and not fret how it will affect us." He chuckled again. "Have I not already assured Demicolon and Pseudofluff that their future postage would not be turned away... *under oath*, no less? I would say we are all bound by duty here... as we should be.

It doesn't altogether make what we have to do easy... but at least it gives us a sure course."

* * *

They departed the General's office, with Horus feeling ironically to be in a worse predicament than before. Rutherford's gracious way of absolving him of any guilt only served to confirm the guilt was there. Yes, as a Public Defender, he had to do what was best for his client. But since when did that require him to be complicit with devious prosecutors? And what of his other duties? There were just so many external considerations in this case, all impossible to reconcile. Where exactly *was* the highest justice to be served, and why couldn't he seem to lock onto it? Where was that 'sure course' the General had mentioned? What was he missing?

He was soon to get some relief from these questions... indeed, quite a bit more than he would've bargained for. As he returned to the lobby of the Postal Headquarters, the storm outside wrested his attention dramatically from the storm within. In the time it took for Rutherford and him to leave the office wing, the rain had gone from merely torrential to borderline-allegorical. He didn't know how long he stood there, just watching the deluge... his mind finally and totally blank. He was hopeless to solve the case. He couldn't even decide whether to take another step...

He felt something nudge him in the side.

He looked down...

"You appear to have come without parasol," Rutherford observed. "Please, take mine."

The General held out an umbrella to Horus, which appeared only slightly larger than what he might find in a fancy fruit drink with a bendy straw. He was very slow to accept it... both because it was such an incredibly undeserved act of kindness, and because he knew it would do someone of his girth absolutely no good...

"If you're sure. I hate to deprive you."

"Quite sure." He shook the umbrella insistently.

"Very well," Horus said, taking it. "Thank you, General."

"Far be it from me to deny a kindred spirit any kindness. Creatorspeed, Horus Templar."

* * *

The mad dash back to the bungalow was a blur, and not just because he couldn't hope to really keep his eyes open. More than half the time, it felt like he was swimming rather than running. In the end, Rutherford's umbrella may well have been enough to keep his left ear passably dry. The rest of him was soaked through... cold and tender to the point where it felt like the bones in his feet were bruising their way into jellified skin...

Coming up on his place at last, he went to throw the door open, only to find it locked. He cursed under his breath as he fumbled for the keys, wondering why in creation Jether would've locked the door. He almost didn't notice the note left behind, in runny ink:

"Gone to the gym to practice flying. Back whenever."

Horus ripped the note off the door even as he finally pushed in...

It took a few minutes just to calm down enough to collect himself a bit. He was surly and bedraggled – somewhat lost in an adrenaline-fueled fluster to get warm and dry. He shook his whole pelt out, for what good it did in his full, heavy suit. He rooted around rather destructively for anything like a towel, removing his upper garments, lamenting he had no changes of pants packed. Then he remembered there was a fireplace. He worked numb fingers to get something going, fumbling angrily with the flint until a spark finally caught. And, just when he might've settled down and started the long process of drying his outer layers and thawing his inner ones, there was a knock at the door...

He ground his sharp teeth around in his mouth as he marched, mumbling various nothings he meant to hurl at his aide...

He flung the door, and the hurling was on...

"*Darn it*, Jether, why couldn't you just...?"

But it wasn't Jether.

It was Deborah.

"Horus," she said.

"Deborah," he answered. "I... I'm surprised to see you."

She shrugged. "Yeah, well, the tradeshow got washed out. Thought maybe I'd make that visit I promised the other day."

Washed out? Oh yes... it was raining. She was standing in front of him in a full rain jacket and umbrella. Still outside, in the downpour...

"Oh, of course, come in!" he bolted.

"If you're sure," she replied. "I can always wait until you're dressed."

Horus was finally aware of himself. He wore only his soggy pants and a small towel over his shoulders. His ears folded back, and he snickered. "Well, suppose you let yourself in anyway, and I run back upstairs and grab a shirt?"

* * *

It took a bit of creativity with blankets and boxes of still-unpacked case reports to improvise something of a couch, but before long, they were huddled by a quiet fire, trying not to look too desperate to warm their extremities. Horus' legs felt like dead stumps set into a river basin. Deborah was in better shape, but even with all her smart outfitting, her shoes, tights, and the hem of her skirt were still soaked. For quite a while, they just sat without speaking. Horus was almost too comforted by her presence to want to spoil it by catching up...

"How's the case been going, Boss?" Deborah asked at length.

Horus mustered a confident grin. "Splendidly, thank you."

She grimaced. "That bad, huh?"

He slouched, looking evasively back into the fire. "I admit, there's been a time or two I would've greatly appreciated your insight. Things have been... a bit trying."

They were quiet for a moment. "This hasn't been easy for me either, you know," Deborah admitted. "Just force-feeding myself that awful cereal is like torture."

Surprising himself, he chortled. "What? You mean to tell me you *don't like it*?"

She smiled, and swatted at him. "Shut up."

"Sorry," he chuckled, holding up defensive hands. "Believe me, I wish something could be done about your new job, beyond just making light of it."

"So do I," she nodded.

They settled back into an uncomfortable silence.

"Maybe it's better if we focus on your business," Deborah rejoined. "What've you been having trouble with?"

"Where to even begin?" Horus sighed. "Suffice it to say, the Viziers are obliged to uphold Dominion over citizenship. From the very first session, the prosecutors have had full steerage. One or the other will prevail in the end... that much I fear is inevitable. It's just a question of how best to optimize the defeat now."

Deborah patted him on the shoulder. "Poor Mo. He must be devastated."

"Hm?" Horus responded, as if her reaction was almost a non-sequitur. "Ah, well, perhaps not," he dismissed it. "He does seem to feel he was owed some punishment." He lingered on this point a while, stewing. "Actually, he turned down a work release I arranged for him. Turned it down flat."

"That's strange," Deborah replied, sounding more unsure than puzzled.

"Strange," Horus agreed. "Inconvenient. Downright frustrating. He doesn't seem to appreciate how important it is that I help him. Someone like me *has to* help someone like him, at some point. Someone needs to set the right example... and the sooner, the better."

"I'm... I'm not sure what you're getting at," she confessed.

"Well surely you see it," he suggested. "The opportunity here, Deborah. The opportunity to put the past where it belongs. The opportunity for a Mesomela to perform an exceptional kindness to an ancient enemy... to a *Berlie Beirel*... just as if everything they did doesn't matter anymore. To let such a chance simply elude me... after having it handed to me on a silver platter... it's a travesty." He rolled his fingers thoughtfully under his chin. "But then, maybe it was never in my power to set a meaningful precedent to begin with. I suppose, in the end, it proves nothing if *I* forgive him. My family didn't watch as Aedeloma razed our last cities. They were already long gone by then. That's no secret. People will be sure to dig it up. It wouldn't be the first time." He ran his hands over his head and ears, bewildered. "Why did it have to be like this? Why did I have to prove so inadequate, right when victory was most vital? I doubt anyone will ever know I even tried. Why, after all, should any Mesomela wish to help a Berlie Beirel?"

"Horus, you're being a hypocrite."

He blinked.

Slowly, he turned to face her. "I'm... I'm *what*?"

"You're being a hypocrite," Deborah reiterated. "You say all that ancient stuff makes no difference to you... yet there wasn't a single thing you just said that didn't invoke the 770 Years War."

Horus was taken aback. His eyes flitted as if searching back through a transcript of the thoughts he'd just voiced. To his greater amazement, she was right...

"I... but I don't mean to..."

"You don't owe me any explanation, Horus," she assured him. "I know what you went through... with your father and uncle, and all. How could you not want to distance yourself from that? How could you not want to push back against the kind of senseless hatred they got mixed up in? But I think you're overcorrecting. I think, in a way, you're making the same mistake they did. You're making the same mistake the Czarina made by putting Aphelo on trial for the whole Mantid species. You can't make this about representing a *Berlie Beirel* – you have to represent *Mo*. You owe him that. You owe that to yourself. This case has got you feeling all mixed up – I can see that. You're just not quite yourself. And I hate to say it, but I think you'll *keep* feeling mixed up... until you're clear about who you're representing, and why."

For a moment, Horus marveled at her. This was the Deborah he was so fond of, at her very best. Such wisdom... such gentle reproach. Up until now, he'd always been guarded when it came to talking about Berlie Beirels around Deborah... excepting the time he'd told her about the saga with his father and uncle. He'd always feared to discover some of that same old prejudice in her, if he pursued the subject too much. But now, in this most remarkable way, he'd discovered she had a clear head on her shoulders about the whole thing all along. Even clearer, it turned out, than his own...

"Well, I'll be," he said, grinning as he shook his head. "How did I ever let something so simple become so complicated?"

She shrugged. "Beats me, Boss."

All at once, she got a surprised look on her face, and went rummaging for her handbag. "Oh, before I forget, I've got something for you." She found something small and shiny, and flipped it at him. He barely managed to catch it...

"What is it?" he asked before even venturing a look.

"Penny for your thoughts, I guess," she answered. "I got to spend a little time rooting around the rest of the trade show. Nothing much stuck out... except for this one crazy coin-stamping booth."

"*Really*?" Horus wondered with a smile. "Isn't that something? I know exactly the one you're talking about! It struck me, too, thinking how illegal something like that would be in Jast-Madiir."

"My thoughts exactly," she nodded. "Go ahead and look at it."

He finally worked the little coin out of the flats of his palms and into his fingers. Raising it and turning it so the fire revealed the relief, he saw that it had a simple smiley face imprinted onto it...

"That's for any time I can't be there to give you a smile myself," she said. "At least until the return trip. That *was* one of our shillings… I wouldn't recommend trying to get it through customs, if I were you."

"And yet how I'll hate to part with it," he said, grinning rather stupidly back at the coin. "Even so, I may have to see if I can get a local grocer to take it long before that. Thanks to my aide – the boy-wonder – and the rather expensive contents of this couch, money is in short supply these days."

She gave him a sympathetic look. "Bit of a nuisance, is he?"

"He's running me ragged," Horus admitted.

"You *do* have some monster bags under your eyes," she said. "Still not sleeping well, either?"

"Not especially."

She got up. "Have you got any ankylosaur eggs? I'll mix some up in a cup for you. You're always better after a good swig of egg."

"I think there might be one or two plesiosaur eggs left. It's a job, trying to find any sort of dino eggs at all in the local markets. For some reason, they don't seem to be widely regarded as foodstuff in this country."

"I can't imagine," she replied sarcastically. "Do you want me to make them up?"

He nodded. "Something to perk me up a bit might be in order. This isn't the best time for me to be drowsy. There's quite a lot left to sort out. Hopefully, with the help of your gracious insights, I can finally begin to chart a clear path forward."

"Don't worry," she assuaged him. "You still have room to do what you always do. Your very best."

Chapter 14

There it sat... right in front of him. Or, perhaps it *stood*. He found himself suddenly wondering: Are chairs really considered to be *sitting*, or are they merely sat upon? He shook his head. What a strange thing to wonder, here and now, confronted by his worst nightmare – its terrible wooden legs resting on unsettling wispy dream essence – its cushion so totally and horribly devoid of occupancy...

"Well, here we are again," he dared to speak at the object of his dread. "What can I do but accept it? No matter what I do, I'll never be able to get anyone to sit on you."

"Oy, but you shouldn't let that trouble you none, Mr. Templar, Sir," a voice said, from off to his right. He turned... and there, to his surprise, was Mobipetrolluck...

"...Some of us prefer to float."

ACHOO! Horus sneezed, blasting his brain back to consciousness. Once there, he was thoroughly displeased to find Jether in his face, holding a plucked feather out in front of his snout. He reflexively tried to wiggle the tickly feeling out of his nostrils...

"Jether!" he demanded. "What in the Undervoid do you think you're doing?!"

"You were asleep, Mr. Templar," the lad explained. "So I woke you up."

"What perfectly reductive logic," he quipped. However, upon further review, he was rather struck by one of these obvious truths. "But then, you're right... I really *was* asleep. What's more... I actually think I might've stayed that way..." He sat up very straight, ears equally rigid as he scanned the room... another thought pressing suddenly on him. "Deborah was here," he recalled aloud.

"Your secretary?"

"Yes," he answered, never breaking his search pattern. "She had some leisure when the trade show got washed out. Where did she go?"

"The rain's stopped, Mr. Templar... or I wouldn't be here now. She must've gone back. 'The show must go on,' and all that stuff."

Horus couldn't help feeling he'd cheated himself. Evidently, Deborah's visit had been a little too reassuring. In the time it took for her to rummage a bit in the kitchen area, he'd dozed off. When every chance he got to see her could be his last, sleeping through such an occasion was far from ideal. He suppressed the urge to curse...

"...Anyway, you've got *me*, so any sound advice you might be looking for going into tomorrow is readily available," Jether continued.

"Your advice has been terrible," Horus replied. "You've thought entirely about what's cool, and not at all about what's right."

Jether nodded. "The exact opposite of what you do. That's what makes us good counterparts." He cocked his head. "What did your secretary have to say that's so special?"

"Quite a lot, considering the limited time," Horus said, reflecting deeply on it all, while he settled back into thinking-aloud mode. "She said I haven't been myself. Who am I, if not myself?"

"Oh, you're you alright," Jether assured him. "No one else I know spends so much time hurdling through these kinds of meaningless questions."

"She accused me of making this whole case about the 770 Year's War... and she was right," Horus continued, ignoring him. "Mostly, I've either been thinking about how to patch the schism between Mesomelae and Berlie Beirels, or I've been fretting about..." he caught himself, "...about uncertainties. I've been ruminating over a past that's already gone... and a future that might never come at all. I haven't been *present.* There's a client who needs my help right now, and I haven't so much as learned a thing about him, much less how to represent his interests..."

He stood, feeling he'd reached something of an epiphany. "*He's* my empty chair. I've neglected him. I've actively avoided him..." He whirled, facing Jether with the full radiance of enlightenment. "I'm... I'm *my own* empty chair!"

"Sounds like just a lot of wandering sentimentalism to me," Jether admitted.

Horus reached for his jacket hanging by the fire, snatching it from the rack. "The word you're looking for is *psychiatry,* my boy," he said, throwing the jacket on as he made for the door.

"Where are you going now?" the young Heron asked impatiently.

"Isn't it obvious?" Horus replied. "It's high-time I had a talk with my client. A bonified, honest-to-goodness talk..."

* * *

"So that's the long and short of it, Mo," Horus said, holding a cup on a string to his mouth, while his other thumbnail absently traced the edges of the coin Deborah gave him. "You know I don't have a prayer of getting you off scot-free. You know I can get you a light sentence – a single expended life in the military. But you also know the terrible cost, if I can't stop either Demicolon or Pseudofluff carrying out their plan to appeal the Tribunal's decision. So now, I put it to you, my good man... what would you like me to do? How can I best serve your interests, given the limited scope of my power over this whole situation?"

"I want you to let 'em 'ave it, Mr. Templar!" Mo flashed excitedly, holding up the cup on his end of the call they were making through the corrections booth. "Fight it out! Go down swingin', Sir! Someone ought t' stand in the way o' their dastardly deeds! Think of all they've done... all the impossible choices they've left us with... mine, yours... the Viziers'... even poor Rutherford and 'is postmen! Someone 'as to stop them, Sir!"

Horus chuckled at the Clerk's enthusiasm. "Well, I'm glad you feel that way. But you must understand... if I don't deal, they have what amounts to free license to pursue *any* severity of punishment for you. Tophthera and Toefthaera are new nations, whose penalties for draft evasion have no precedent. You may spend the rest of your life a soldier. You may never work for the Dronehood again."

"Rubbish, Sir... beggin' your pardon. You can take the drone out of 'is office, but you can't take the office out o' the drone!" He leaned in toward the glass barrier, as if for discretion. "For instance," he said low, "I 'ave this new scatterplot I've been workin' on! Oh, nothin' extravagant... just a chart for the number o' times a guard passes by me cell ev'ry day. I 'ave to say, the data ranges rather wildly, Mr. Templar! By as many as eleven passes, to date."

"It's good to hear you're keeping in practice," Horus nodded warmly.

"I am, Sir! That I am! And you may rest assured I shan't stop, when they ship me off to her Majesty's service. There's always something to chart, Sir... *always*. That's why it doesn't trouble me to be found guilty. I would've gladly served me Queen from the start, if only I could've been sure who she rightly was. I'll make the most o' me wages, whatever comes. I'll be well-off, whichever way it goes. Only I reckon those prosecutors are guilty as I am. That's why I say: Give 'em the ol' one-two! I warrant they 'ave it comin'."

Horus' nail slipped from the coin's edge. He shook his head, somewhat more grave. "Much as I agree, I also hope you understand that I still see no earthly way of hindering their plans for appeal. I still have my courtroom reflexes... and I still have until tomorrow. I'll make it into a brawl, the best I can. But you shouldn't hope for more than token resistance."

Mo shifted, internal light pulsing as he considered something. "Speakin' o' tokens, Sir... may I ask what denomination you 'ave there, tumblin' in your paw? It don't look so familiar..."

Horus was momentarily flummoxed, until he became conscious of fidgeting with Deborah's coin. "This?" he asked. "It *was* a Jast-Madiir shilling." He held it up for Mo to see clearly. "My secretary had it personalized."

Mo's glow suddenly went solar. "Blimey! A one-of-kind coin! Now, that there, Sir... *that* would be something to chart!"

Horus' brow knit. "Oh? How does one chart a coin?"

"The *flips*, Sir!" Mo explained. "Recordin' how many times it lands on one side, versus the other. The Drone'ood 'as very extensive flip-stats on ev'ry kind o' coin there ever was! Did you know, Mr. Templar, that the trites used right in this very country are the only coins t' boast a true flip ratio of 1:1... to within a ten-thousandth of a percent?!"

Horus remained unsure. "But aren't Roemnari trites unstamped? They have no relief design whatsoever..."

"Precisely, Sir!" Mo agreed. "That's why they're so reliable. Their sides 'ave almost perfect weight distribution!"

"Yes," Horus nodded. "The sides are identically flat. But that being the case, how do you keep track of which side lands up or down?"

"We just marked 'em up with ink, Sir. Any two dissimilar designs would do. Two numbers, two letters, two different colors..."

Horus blinked. He dropped his coin, prompting him to lose the cup as well when he stooped to scramble on the ground for it. Fortunately, he was able to find the smiley coin in short order. He admired it in his grasp, eyes fighting back moisture as he resolved... this would be his last good look at it...

"Bit of clumsiness there, Mr. Templar," Mo extended his understanding, once Horus had also taken the cup back up. "Are you quite alright?"

"Much better than alright, Mo," he replied. "Tell me: You wouldn't happen to have a Roemnari trite on your person, would you?"

"Matter of fact I do," the Clerk confirmed. "I 'ad to spend a few to place this call."

"In that case, I propose we arrange a trade," Horus said, holding the smiley coin out to him again. "One for one. My unique shilling for one of your trites."

"Are you quite sure, Sir?" Mo gasped. "The exchange rate is *not* in your favor!"

"Oh, *it is*," Horus assured him. "You needn't worry about shorting me. I had to be rid of this coin eventually... suffice it to say, it's no longer legal tender. It was... a meaningful gift. Now it will be again. Besides, I think you'll be amazed how far I can stretch a single trite."

Mo flashed with confusion. "I can't imagine what you mean."

"You'll see, Mo. Soon, you'll see. This exchange is in *both* our favors."

* * *

It was all Horus could do not to skip out of the detention block, back onto those beautiful, featureless stone streets and the frigid night air. He'd finally acquainted himself with the remarkable person of his client, and emerged from the meeting inspired – revived – sure of his path. The world was right again...

...Or anyway, it was much righter than it had been.

He reached into his pocket, pulling out the trite... tumbling it around... his fingers remembering the shilling he'd traded for it with a tender yearning, as if they'd known and cradled it for years. And he thought. He thought on his one remaining uncertainty. He thought of the lady who'd given it to him...

Then, coin still in hand, he found himself looking down both ends of the street. One way led back to his bungalow. The other continued on to the medical facility where Nokkaeru was put up. Nokkaeru – the doctor who could arrange his meeting with the Proconsul. The doctor who held the cure to what ailed him... the means to answer all the dark questions of his future...

...With one question before all others...

Would that smile be his to enjoy again?

For a long while, he deliberated. He searched along each path with eyes and mind for what seemed like ages. And he studied the trite... half-minded to use it to divine his answers now...

He sighed.

"We don't have many assurances in life," he told himself. "I can try to circumvent that. But perhaps it's better if I just learn to live with it."

He put the trite back in his pocket.

And quietly, without another thought, he headed home...

Chapter 15

Deciding this might be as good a night as any for a little sleep, Blucille had scarcely settled-in when she heard a knock at her door...

Well, this is it, she thought. There was no legitimate reason for anyone to come calling now. Being a prominent law official, she'd already worked out that an attack from the Cults was an eventuality. This was a bit earlier in the game than she might've expected... but after all, she'd been snooping around their school. By this time, they probably even knew she'd been coordinating the SAPD's efforts against them since the earliest plans to embed a double-agent...

She made some grumpy noises and went for the crowbar under her pillow...

The door creaked as she opened it with one hand, holding the crowbar up behind her ears with the other, ready to whop the first Cultist who made a move. To her surprise, however, there was only one Cultist on her stoop. A timid little woman, at that. Blucille's steely expression melted into something akin to disappointment...

"What are you doing here?" she asked.

The poor, silly little creature's eyes bugged at the mere question, and she looked ready to bolt. "My..." she stammered, "my name is Teresa."

Blucille nodded. "I know who you are. What do you want? Are you really the best the Cults could come up with for an assassin?"

Teresa shook her head. "I'm not here to kill you, Miss," she explained. "I'm here about Art..."

Blucille's brow rose.

Finally, she lowered the crowbar, using it to gesture into her foyer...

"In that case, come in."

* * *

SHWRRRLP

Blucille began the meeting with a swift tug on the large retractable map. The crisp sound of the sheet made for a worthy punctuation mark, but in point of fact, a rather unnecessary one. The room full of cops and soldiers was already taught with eager silence – she had their full attention before any attempt was made to demand it. It wasn't that they grudged her this second night-raid. Rather, they were hungry for the victory they'd been denied at the schoolhouse. They were confident, and they were solemn. Most of all, they were ready...

"Welcome back to the night shift, gentlemen," Blucille said, pulling out on a collapsible pointer. "I'm sure there's no need to review the basics. You know why we're here. You know who we're up against. For months now, we've let these Cultists outfox and outmaneuver us. But no more. This time, we have the drop on them. Tonight, we prove they're not as strong or as clever as their boasting. Tonight, with one swift stroke, we end their ilk for good." She turned her head, nodding at Captain Alexei. "Acting Constable," she acknowledged him.

He took a few long but regimented strides forward, clicking heels together as he faced his men. "Before we begin the briefing in earnest, you may as well be assured that we're acting on inside information. My esteemed colleague here has just received the deposition of a known Cultist." He paused a beat. "We have learned the whereabouts of their secret leader."

At this, the otherwise razor-focused assembly could hardly help breaking into hushed murmurs of amazement. Alexei gave them a moment to digest his revelation.

"Yes, this really *is* for all the marbles, my good fellows. Our principal object, therefore, should be no mystery. We must have *the leader*. All other concerns are secondary. Gladly, I may report that he should be easy to pick out of the crowd. He is not at all as we might've pictured him. His name is Sabracore... and he is Meduseldan."

This elicited more murmurs... and more than a few faces soured with unbelief. Alexei held up a hand...

"I know how it sounds... believe me, I do. The Assistant District Attorney and I were not quick to accept this point, either. But after careful examination of our witness, we are satisfied that her testimony is in earnest. If nothing else, perhaps it will begin to alleviate your fears to mention that this Sabracore is also a Wuu Gappew."

A third time, the assembly reacted, nodding amongst themselves and generally appearing more hopeful that this made sense.

"In any case, under no circumstances can we permit this villain to escape. He alone holds the true power of the Cults to sway our friends and neighbors. You must above all be on the lookout for him... and you must be *wary*. You are to remain in groups of three or four at all times. If you engage him, you must immediately confiscate any and all pocket watches on his person. These precautions may sound strange, but they are critical to the safety and security of your minds."

Alexei nodded back at Blucille, surrendering the floor. She surveyed the room. "This is an extremely delicate operation we're about to undertake," she explained. "I know your frustrations, and I share them. I share your eagerness to uphold the sovereignty of the Czarina, which the Cults have threatened. However, we must exercise care not to unduly harm the general rank-and-file Cultists. These are still economically viable citizens we're talking about. They've held down their jobs and state obligations... thus far. As such, they are to be treated as any other heretics. Their rehabilitation will be in the capable hands of the Inquisition..." She gestured across the room, where an Inquisitor representative was standing. He nodded. "They are to be arrested and processed," she continued. "Use lethal force only where necessary. And..." she paused, her voice softening a little, in spite of herself, "...keep an eye out for a Mesomela man answering to the name of Art Mallard. He is one of our operatives, whose cover has been compromised. With any luck, it won't be too late to liberate him from their influence."

Slowly, she turned, mustering gumption again as she approached the big map she'd earlier revealed. She pointed at it with her pointer...

"This, then, is where Sabracore and his lackeys are put up."

She moved the pointer, striking the map in a second place.

"And – *this* – is where we will begin our assault."

* * *

Every time Art moved even a little, he was overwhelmed with dizziness. The effects of Sabracore's merciless assaults on his few remaining mental defenses were becoming more acute all the time, and lingering longer and longer after each session. Apart from the vertigo, he knew only exhaustion. Complete and utter exhaustion. Not just from being kept up for who-knows-how-long, and not just from resisting with all his brain-power. Even these moments of respite in his cell were taking a huge toll. He would lie awake – or partly awake – fretting about which memories and experiences of his were true, and which had been twisted, or even forgotten altogether. He couldn't trust his own inventory anymore... but that didn't stop him constantly taking it. There was nothing else. Or, if there was anything else, it was only the insurmountable sense that it was all hopeless... that he might as well surrender. It was a feeling that grew exponentially every time he came up against it. No wonder, then, that it was all he could do to retreat into the treacherous bog of his memories. He was running himself ragged just to keep ahead of the inevitable a little longer...

It was as he rubbed his eyes hard and groaned again in the dregs of his despair that he detected outside stimulus... hushed voices in the hall. Goons were out there, keeping what they must've believed was private council. But Art could hear every word. As he listened, he was astonished from the very first. He heard... *uncertainty*... in their voices. Even fear...

"What's going on out there?" one Goon inquired. "What's all the fuss about?"

"It's *cannon fire*!" the other replied in a strained whisper. "A dozen guns or more!"

Art blinked. Sure enough, a rumbling he must've dismissed as distant thunder pressed on his awareness. *Cannon fire?* he thought. *What could that mean...?*

"Impossible!" the first Goon insisted. "Get a hold of yourself, friend. Why, I'm sure it's only a storm."

"But I've been topside! I saw it myself! The warehouse two doors down is being shelled to pieces! You'll smell the smoke for yourself, if they get any closer!"

Art sniffed the air, hoping for smoke.

"What're we going to do?" the first Goon seemed to break down. "Surely Sabracore will order an evacuation..."

"I think he's minded to wait and see," the second Goon explained. "The Czarina is onto us, it seems... but she's missed her mark. It's all a matter of trying to read her next play. If they start blasting another warehouse, then we'll know they're going right down the line. We'll be off on a run! But if they stop, we might be better served to hunker down. It could be they're just hitting warehouses at random... or else they got the wrong one entirely."

"It's too close for comfort, either way. I wish we'd up and go now, while the getting's good!"

"The Bishop disagrees. We'll wait until we have another sign. They're still two warehouses over. There's still plenty of time."

"I hope you're right."

Art was perhaps a little too lost in the landslide of new data to feel sick with dizziness anymore. He sat up, reflecting on it all. What were the odds of such an attack, so nearby? How could the police have learned he was put up in a warehouse... unless Teresa had told them? But if she had, then *how* could they get the address wrong? That didn't seem at all like the SAPD. They tended to pay attention to those kinds of details...

Finally, it hit him like a freight train... a horrible, bitter freight train. This was obviously just another trick... a ruse to get him even more mixed up, just like that first bogus police-raid stunt, or that time he thought he'd been speaking to... to a lady-friend whose name was sadly not forthcoming at present. Classic Sabracore theatrics! Anyway, why else would a pair of Goons be talking about such things, right within earshot of his cell?

Oh, they're good, he thought. *But not as good as they give themselves credit for. If they think I'm going to believe the next cop I see for a moment, they've got another thing coming...*

Like maybe a judo-chop and a mad dash...

* * *

Blucille and Alexei looked on as a healthy dose of cannonade immolated their target. Though they were forced to cover their ears – and even then, found the din of the barrage uncomfortable – they had little trouble fixing smug grins on their faces for the duration...

When the foundations of the warehouse had been laid bare, Captain Leonards of the artillery unit appeared, begging new orders...

"There's little more we can do here, Sir and Ma'am," he explained. "We're just wasting shells on rubble at this point. Shall we continue on to the next target?"

The acting Deputy Constable and the ADA exchanged looks. "I believe this is chiefly your operation, Ms. Cordon," Alexei said. "It's your call."

She turned to Leonards. "Very well. You may give the order to move on."

* * *

Just listen to them out there, Art told himself, shaking his head. *What a show they must think they're putting on! A whole hornet's nest set buzzing, properly spooked! But I know better, don't I? Heh! Why, they're no better than bunch of chuckleheads running around, too dumb to know when they've pushed the envelope too far...*

"What is it *now*?" a Goon asked, just beyond his door, not even trying to be discrete anymore.

"We've been ordered to evacuate," the other Goon replied. "They've started shelling the warehouse just across from us!"

"What about the prisoner?"

"The Bishop wants him brought."

"Does he *really*? Why not just kill him and be done with it? He'll only slow us down."

"Au contrary," Art put in, sticking his nose through the bars of his window. "I don't want nothin' to do with those no-good coppers," he claimed, if only for the satisfaction of seeing how his unexpected reaction would tend to hamper them. "I'll gladly come along with the Bishop."

He watched them look at him stupefied, deeply enjoying every moment of it. Finally, one Goon looked back at the other.

"Do you think he's serious?"

He shrugged. "He seems to be."

The Goon turned back. "Alright. No time to second-guess the Bishop anyhow. You're coming with us."

* * *

The orchestrators of the sting operation didn't wait around to see the next warehouse go up in a ball of fire and raining bricks. Rather, they continued on their way, embedding in the shadows with the rest of the police force, backed up by the infantry. Through neat little binoculars, they watched as the Cultists began to pour quietly out of their actual hideout, little suspecting that while the warehouse a few hundred yards over erupted into dramatic pyrotechnics, the *real* body of law enforcement was waiting silently in ambush for them. Sneaky as they tried to be, somewhere between 50 and 100 Cultists walked right into the hands of cops stationed all around the perimeter before there was any sign they knew that they'd been had. The first Cultist to turn back hollering triggered a massed advance by the encircling police. They would push now, before their enemies had a chance to change tactics and fortify. Under heavy escort, Cordon and Alexei moved in with the attack...

* * *

"We've brought the prisoner," a Goon explained as they entered the Bishop's Sanctum.

"Hey, Bishop," Art greeted Sabracore with a friendly wave. "Some shakeup, eh? I sure didn't see *this one* coming."

Sabracore fairly ignored him, turning to Overseer Therodrux, as if inviting a status report.

"There's no time to waste confusing matters," Therodrux obliged him. "We'll have to hope they destroy any meaningful evidence with their own cannons. But we have to get you out *now*."

"Agreed," the Bishop replied.

But just as he began to float onward, he stopped, unsure. An all-too familiar clatter echoed into the room from the stairway at the other end of the hall: scuffling, and a distant shot. Art barely kept himself from snickering. The Bishop's subtlety really *had* run its course. This was practically an exact redo of the first time they'd pulled one over on him!

And so it continued to play out. Just like before, Therodrux ordered his personal entourage to advance first, as if to clear the way for them. And as before, they complied with a horrified look. Perhaps they all hoped the sheer sense of déjà vu alone would push Art over the edge of his sanity. But if that's what they expected, they were a far sight off indeed...

Art crossed his arms as he listened to the charade wind down to its predictable conclusion, grinning all the while in his knowing. He heard the Goons wrestled down and subdued. He listened as Therodrux made laughable appeals to a last-ditch effort to hide Sabracore in his own Sanctum. And finally, he watched as 'cops' and even a few 'soldiers' poured into the room. He had to admit, the pageantry was impressively expanded this time around. But he still didn't buy it...

"Freeze!" a 'police lieutenant' demanded, leveling a service pistol at Therodrux.

"Dianodes, there's the jelly... just like the captain said!" another exclaimed. "Nab him! Don't let him go for those pocket-watches..."

"Hey there," yet another officer said, taking Art at unawares as he grabbed him by the arm. "Your name Art Mallard by any chance?"

"Sure is," Art smiled, big and toothy. Then he slugged the 'copper' a good one right in the nose and bolted!

The general commotion was just perfect. None of the phony policemen had expected him to punch his way out! They were all too busy putting on their silly act of apprehending the Bishop to react in time. He blew through the door and slammed it behind him!

...But just as he was about to wind-sprint up and away to whatever reality awaited him beyond the walls of that loathsome warehouse, an obstacle of no small familiarity appeared right in his way...

Art stopped-up dead in his tracks.

Both he and she stood utterly frozen, searching each other with mirrored expressions of incredulity...

"Art?" the lady asked.

Art didn't reply at once. His mind was locked in a channel of trying to come up with a name for this lovely face and hat. He knew it. He *knew* he knew it...

"Blucille?" he asked in return. And suddenly it all seemed to come back to him. She wasn't quite as he remembered her... but something just clicked all the same. And the longer he studied her, the more he believed. Maybe... just maybe... it really *could* be her...

He reached out, running his hands along her face to be sure...

"Your voice sounds funny..." he mused aloud, "...but your head seems real enough."

She swatted at his hands. "Don't do that."

Art was genuinely amazed. There was an authenticity about her annoyance that resonated. Moreover, he sniffed, and his nostrils were filled with an old fragrance...

"What is that?" he inquired, drawing a momentary blank as he took a second sniff. "*Lavender*?"

She nodded – confused, perhaps with a hint of shame. Art's face lit up...

"By golly, it really *is* you!" And without a moment's thought, he hugged her.

For her part, Blucille found herself in a temporary paralysis. His reaction was... well... rather nice. Unexpected, overblown... but nice. At length, she reached up and patted the big lug on the shoulder. "I'm... I'm sorry it took so long to find you, Art," she said.

"Long?" he asked. He drew her out of his own hug, arms still on her shoulders. "How long *has* it been? Did... did we miss *Friday*?"

Her jowls settled into another mystified frown. "I guess they really have been messing with your head. Well, hopefully it's not too late to fill most of the potholes back in..."

"*Ahem,*" Captain Alexei put in. He and several officers had been present all along. "I hate to intrude, but any reeducating of Mr. Mallard will have to be for later."

"Hey, I know you, too," Art said, taking notice of him. "...At least, I think I do."

"You do," Alexei nodded. "But as I said, there's no time to bring you back up to speed now. We have other business."

"Yes," Blucille agreed. "It's high-time we paid our respects to this Bishop Sabracore..."

"Well wait," Art stopped them up. "How did you find me, anyway? Was it Teresa?"

"It was," Blucille answered.

"Is she here now!?" Art insisted.

"She is." Blucille and Alexei alike were unsure. "We always bring the mole along for the sting. It's one of the best things we can do to discourage misinformation. But what does...?"

"...Can you have her brought down here?" Art cut her off. "I think she should get to see this..."

* * *

The time finally came for the Captain and ADA to bag their prize. Lieutenants and infantrymen poured into the Sanctum before and after them, until it was all-but a packed house. There was no question as to the identities of the suspects within. There was one Human – undoubtedly Therodrux – though he didn't closely match Art's doodle. Perhaps it was the absence of his smug smile. And, beside him, there was a Meduseldan, all in dark layers of cloak. Their true adversary: the Bishop himself...

But before they could confront him personally, Therodrux cut in...

"So you've caught me at last... the Supreme Elevated Grand Master Overseer of the Digit Cults!" he announced, a bit too emphatically. "I confess! I throw myself at the mercy of your Czarina! All I ask is that you would turn your wrath aside from those I've held captive here, including this humble Clerk." He indicated Sabracore. "Truly, an innocent bystander, if ever there was one..."

"Save it, Therodrux," Sabracore reprimanded his pupil. "They know better than that, or they wouldn't have taken my watches. No lies you tell now will suffice to protect the truth." He turned and regarded his captors. "So this is Blucille Cordon and Alexei of Podunkville," he greeted them. "I do admit to being a bit stymied. If our Initiative was doomed to this very minor setback, then at least we could've been interned by the top brass. Oh, I understand the Deputy Constable has other appointments to keep. My condolences. But I might've at least met Hamilton Blackforest. Still, all in good time, I suppose..."

"I don't think so," Blucille replied, folding her arms. "The District Attorney has bigger fish to fry than you, Sabracore. *Real* hardened criminals. Loiterers... jaywalkers. He trusts me to eat the small potatoes like you for breakfast. And that's just what I intend to do."

Sabracore tsked at her. "So conceited. But I admit: You've won this round. I only want to know one thing. How? What gave us away?"

Blucille grinned. "One of your own, Bishop. It was one of your own."

Sabracore answered with a brooding silence. Finally, he laughed it off airily. "Nice try," he said. "Very good delivery. But then, lying is the business you're in. Come now, what was it *really*? What harm could it do to tell me now?"

She shook her head. "You're not getting it. You were ratted out. Though, to call the little lady a rat would be unfair."

"Impossible," the Bishop declared, the level tone of his voice betraying his incredulity. "All who come to this place are reformed by my teaching – destroyed and remade. There's no deceit left in them. No duplicity at all. They are *mine*."

Blucille gestured back at the door. "Apparently, not this one."

Teresa stepped through the threshold on cue, bewildering Sabracore no less than she had Art, only a few days back...

The Bishop flashed brilliantly as his mind reeled. "I don't believe it," he said. "I've bent hundreds of minds to my will – minds greater than hers. She is weak. She's always been weak..."

"That's your failing, Sabracore," Art said, just as he came into the room behind Teresa. "You think you've got everyone figured. But you're only looking at the surface of things. What Teresa here lacks in stature, she makes up for with a big heart. Now I grant you: Retraining the mind... that's one thing. But retraining the *spirit*... well, that's just too big a job for you."

Sabracore's inner light glowered, but he could say nothing.

"Take him away," Blucille instructed at last. The cops threw him in a sizable collection of cuffs and started leading him off...

"This isn't over," the Bishop boded as he wriggled against his restraints. "I have very powerful friends. The truth always comes out, in the end."

"You bet it does," Art replied confidently. Then he gave Sabracore a wink and a thumbs-up as he passed by. "Catch ya on the flipside."

Chapter 16

Horus awakened the following morning from his first undisturbed sleep in weeks… fit and well-rested. His head was clear, his whiskers and ears were spruce, and there was a new spring in the pads of his feet. He couldn't be sure, of course, but he fancied it felt rather like coming back from the dead.

After a comb and a bit of tussling his tie into its proper shape, he had time for a sparse but delicious breakfast. Seeing very little reason to wait up for Jether, he set off immediately to the Tribunal…

On his way out the door, though, he found a mysterious letter – its return address conspicuously absent. Retrieving it, he momentarily retired back to the bungalow's study. He unsealed the envelope with a sharp claw and had the letter unfolded in no time, skipping over the content in favor of learning who the thing was from. He frowned a puzzled frown, seeing it was only signed, "Yours truly, An Associate." This sent him impatiently scanning back through the substance of the letter…

Apparently, it was meant as an anonymous tip… a prompt to examine his case within the context of an obscure international law known as Charion's Statute. At this, Horus found himself scratching his head. He had only the vaguest recollection of the Statute… some zonal technicality that had something to do with 50 feet underground, or some-such. But after a few failed attempts to make heads or tails of the suggestion, he quickly realized there was nothing to do but dismiss it altogether. The case had already defaulted to being about Dominion; even if he had time to familiarize himself thoroughly with Charion's Statute, any further attempts to shoehorn matters back into nationality loopholes would be pointless. Anyway, he *didn't* have time. The case was ending *today,* and he felt it was ending well enough – unsolicited, anonymous tips notwithstanding…

After a hastily convened meeting with the Viziers, Horus returned to his level of the chamber by way of the main entrance. He strode in confident, with scarcely a thought as to the domineering atmosphere of the room. "Good morning, Mo," he said, drawing straight up to his client, greeting him with a genuine smile.

"Mornin', Mr. Templar," Mo replied, looking and sounding a bit uneasy. "I surely 'ope it is to be a good one, against all portents."

"You needn't worry about that," Horus assured him. "We have the odds on our side. An even 50-50."

"I fear you've gone and lost me again, Sir. Aye, but you do look bright-eyed today, I daresay! Like you've got a proper trick up your sleeve!"

"In my pocket, in point of fact. But I'll say nothing more. I'd hate to spoil the surprise."

Just then, Horus spied Jether approaching, a huffy teenage aspect painting his features. "Where were you this morning?" he demanded in a hushed voice. "You could've at least left a note that you weren't waiting up for me."

"I *am* sorry," Horus replied. "There was a diversion that caught me off-guard, and in the end I had to rush ahead. I felt it expedient to bring the Viziers in on my strategy going forward, so I needed to arrive with plenty of time to confer with them."

"*Strategy*?!" Jether asked. "You mean you're still going to try to win this thing?"

"No, not *win*," Horus shook his head. "Rather, I plan to do just as you asked. I'm going to lose classy."

Just then, the piercing sound of the steel gavel rang out over them. "The trial of *Mobipetrolluck vs. The States* is now reconvened," Vizier Arcturus announced. "The prosecution and the prosecution will come forward."

Horus watched as Demicolon and Pseudofluff reclaimed the entryway and the floor – much as they had in the previous convenings – wondering what other acts of arm-twistery they'd committed just to be heralded at the start of every day in court. He shrugged it off. Soon enough, they'd know the fruits of their manipulative ways...

"The defense will now make its case," Vizier Neferib declared, managing tonal indifference. Horus turned up to face them...

"Very well. I would like to proceed immediately to examination."

"You may call your first witnesses," Vizier Serapis allowed.

Horus leveled his gaze back at his opponents. "I call Mr. Demicolon and Mr. Pseudofluff."

The two prosecutors hesitated momentarily, but after gauging each other's reaction, they floated up to the general midst of the witness stand. Once they were settled, Horus went on to pace in front of them...

"I note it as curious... the lack of objection on your parts... being called to testify this way," he began.

"It *is* rather irregular," Demicolon admitted. "But after all, you are within your right. As General Rutherford pointed out, we have been actors in this case since before its inception, in a matter of speaking. Doubtless, you have some wild hope of taking us to task for that."

"No indeed," Horus replied, and it fairly baffled them. "Rather, if I mean to take you to task over anything at all, it would be the private talk the three of us had. The one you arranged between sessions, wherein I was offered a plea deal for my client." He fixed a steely look on them. "Did you not, of your own volition, agree to enforce Mo's enlistment in your armed forces for only a single death? Did you not specify that a mere plea of guilt would earn him this sentence?"

They deferred to each other again briefly. "We did," Pseudofluff answered. "And if you are trying to make a scandal out of it, I would remind you that it is within our *own* right to enforce draft evasion however we see fit... and keep what council we will about establishing the precedent. It is, as you know, the first time any drone has evaded the draft in the history of our new nations."

"I know," Horus agreed. "And I do not mean to imply any scandal. I am only interested in formalizing the agreement here, in open court." Again, he gave them his best stare. "Do you agree to penalize my client with a tour of duty in your armed forces not to exceed a single death?"

"*If* you enter a plea of guilty, here and now," Pseudofluff replied. "Yes."

"We do," Demicolon assented.

Horus nodded. "Very good." He turned back to the Viziers. "In light of this, defense rests its case. It moves to enter a plea of guilty to the charges of draft evasion."

"So entered," Arcturus declared, splitting the air with his gavel. "Mobipetrolluck of the Berlie Beirels, you are hereby found guilty of two counts of draft evasion. You will be taken from this court and forcibly conscripted to the armies. You will serve faithfully up to the time of your death, whereupon you will be returned to your previous duties. The ruling of this Tribunal is final." He struck the gavel again.

Immediately, Demicolon and Pseudofluff were set ablaze with bewilderment. "But... but it is *not* final!" Demicolon demanded. "Your Honors have neglected the most important part! You must choose which Queen he is to serve!"

From this point on, the Viziers were unable to suppress their grins at the prosecutions' expense. "Was I not sufficiently explicit?" Arcturus asked.

"Mobipetrolluck is to serve in both of your armies... first one, and then the other. You have both argued well in favor of your respective Queens. And, so far as we can see, you would seem to have equal claim on this drone. Why not award you both?"

"But you must decide which of us is to receive him *first*!" Pseudofluff insisted urgently. "You must still award precedent!"

The Viziers looked amongst themselves. "Why must we?" Neferib asked. "It is hardly any concern of ours."

"...But if you are quite resolved to have this matter cleared up now," Vizier Serapis continued, looking as if he might be biting back a chuckle, "I believe Mr. Templar is prepared to make a fitting arbitration." He gestured at Horus. "Would you care to take it from here, Counselor?"

"With my thanks, your Honors," Horus nodded. He stroked his chin as he considered each of the prosecutors. "Now, let's see," he said thoughtfully. "Your Asiri certainly seems quite Queenly... but then, Irisa is perhaps no less regal..."

"Your Honors, we vehemently protest!" Demicolon called out. "This is a matter of gravest importance! Surely a mere Public Defender is not equipped to make such a choice!"

"But I *am* equipped," Horus contended. Then he produced a small coin from his pocket. "I have the sure means of a fair decision right here... in the palm of my hand."

They considered it, flashing with outrage. "A *coin*?! But this is outrageous! A legacy as old as the Universe itself is at stake, and you would presume to *flip a coin* on it?!"

"Not just any coin," Horus explained. "A Roemnari trite." He shot a grin back at Mo. "I'm told it's the most impartial coin of them all." He held it up between his fingers, showing both front and back to the prosecutors. "I've inscribed on this particular trite with a permanent marker... 'N' on one side for North, 'S' on the other for South. Simple enough, wouldn't you say?"

"*Simple*?" Demicolon huffed. "I would make it positively naive. *Knavish*, for that matter."

"Even so," Horus shrugged. "You demanded the choice *must* be made. Why be so particular, now it comes to it?"

"Oh, **very well**!" Pseudofluff waved it off. "Go and make your silly toss!"

Horus nodded. He deftly worked the coin up over his thumb, then flipped it off, a satisfying *clink* as his nail struck the silvered copper. He watched its course in the air, as they all did... tracing it until it reached the ground. And, after a few clever little bounces and a bit of lateral rolling (such that Horus knew a moment of doubt, where he feared what would come if the coin defied all the odds and landed on its side!), the trite finally came to rest...

"S," Horus read aloud for the benefit of the court. "Well, that's that!" he summed it up, brushing his hands off. "Mo will serve Asiri first, followed by Irisa."

"No matter!" Demicolon rebutted, throwing the weight of his deep voice around unreservedly now. "What is ruled here today will be of no lasting consequence. I hereby appeal this decision!"

"We both do!" Pseudofluff agreed.

"On what grounds?" Horus asked. "You've already been awarded. How can you possibly appeal a ruling in your favor?" He shook his head. "I don't believe there's any precedent for that."

"Certainly none that applies here," Arcturus interjected. "The case of *Mobipetrolluck vs. The States* is ***closed***. We stand adjourned. Let the defendant be placed in the custody of Mr. Pseudofluff, as per the determination of the coin. That will conclude our present business."

"Perhaps," Demicolon quipped. "But mark these words: We *will* return! We will force this decision, even if we must contrive a hundred other gambits!"

"I'm sure you will," Arcturus replied, as he grabbed his effects and readied to leave his booth. "And we will be waiting for you, each time. With another coin."

Chapter 17

The next day, Horus found himself at the locks, just beyond the moors of a pair of very decrepit-looking vessels. It was the brightest day he'd seen in this strange land, and, perhaps not coincidentally, he knew it would be his last. Not only his, but Mo's as well. And so, he had come to this final bit of irony, where, as his eyes danced over the dark, skeletal ships, he couldn't for the life of him discern which would be heading where...

Fortunately, he didn't agonize long before the whole question conveniently dismissed itself. His ears detecting movement behind him, he turned and found that his client was only now being escorted to the locks himself... one in a mixed train of other Meduselda and a few Héron guards from the local police chapter. Pseudofluff led the whole entourage, of course. He floated right up to Horus, blinking wildly as he grasped for some parting jab. But in the end, he could only turn and waft by without a word. Horus was unaware of any feeling but relief at the parting...

"Come to see me off, Mr. Templar, 'ave you?" Mo called out as he too drew near. "A mighty thoughtful fellow, you are! But I would say your good work is done; you've no need to trouble about *me* anymore!"

"Good morning, Mo," Horus replied. "And don't worry... it's no trouble to come pay my respects. I'll be boarding myself very soon, just a few locks down. But it is good to see you in high spirits."

"Oy, an' why shouldn't I be, Sir?" Mo laughed. "All's well as ends well. And I can scant imagine an 'appier ending than the one you pulled off! Right there in the thick of it, I was – front an' center – when you 'anded those rapscallions the shock of their lives! Oh, it was *poetry*, Mr. Templar – simple an' sweet."

Horus shook his head at the ground, a little embarrassed at all the enthusiasm. "Well, I'm certainly glad you feel so requited. Still, I wonder if I really did you any favors."

Mo was taken aback by this. "But of course you did, Sir! Why, whatever do you mean?"

"Well, don't forget... your sentence has yet to even commence. You're about to face war, Mo... from both sides. I grant that doesn't mean exactly the same for you as it would for me. But it's bound to be an ugly thing."

"For a little while, aye, no doubt it will," Mo agreed more soberly. "But only for a little while. Don't you forget, Mr. Templar... I'm a sight better off than most Clerks what got conscripted. For them, there's no end to the war in sight, an' that's the worst of it. It's them I'm sad for. Meself, I'll be the envy of all the lads. And then I'll be back to the office." He shrugged. "That's all there is for it."

Horus nodded. "You're right, of course. Just as long as you promise me one thing."

"What's that, Sir?"

"Don't let yourself get caught up in it, Mo," he charged him. "The passion, the rivalry, the animosity. Don't let the war master you, as it must've done to the likes of Demicolon and Pseudofluff. I've watched it ruin the kind and unassuming before, as well as the proud and brilliant. That's what I fear most for you."

Mo bobbed solemnly in the air. "Don't fret, Mr. Templar, Sir. I won't soon forget me roots. Anyhow, I've got a scatterplot back 'ome waitin' for me. And I've got your little speech just now. It's enough, Sir. It *will* be enough. Of that I'm sure."

Horus smiled, feeling affirmed. He extended a hand, complete with insulated glove. "I'm glad to have met you, Mo," he said.

"Please, Mr. Templar, call me Lucky," Mo replied as they shook on it. "All me proper friends do."

"Lucky," Horus repeated, nodding. "Perhaps you are after all."

* * *

Not far into Horus' trek to his own ship, the foot-traffic escalated dramatically, and he found himself among as many Humans as Herons, if not more. The trade show was also ending, or at any rate winding-down. He'd done his very best not to keep up on that sphere the last few days, for fear of how it might strike him, if he were to learn that Deborah had already gone ahead on another ship. How exactly the thought of leaving before she did was any better, he couldn't say. Perhaps he could just contrive to imagine that she'd stay on Roemnar... right where he'd left her. Right where he could always find her again. But of course, it was nonsense...

Suddenly, out of the midst of his gloomy thoughts, he spied a visage in the crowd that was known to him. Unfortunately, she spied him right back...

It was Dr. Nokkaeru.

For a moment, he tried to be hopeful... tried to tell himself it might be just any old Plague Doctor... but there were just too many contextual clues.

The adolescent Heron walking beside her, for one... another person he hadn't learned to associate with overly joyful meetings. And then, if that wasn't enough, there was the way she just kept *looking* at him... with goggled eyes so intent, it was as if she believed she could make an anvil drop on his head by sheer force of will...

Finally, with a gentle curse, he decided to veer for her. After all, he *did* need to know how things were going with Miloje. If she was out and about – apparently headed back to their boat – he could only guess the answer wasn't good...

"Hello, Doctor," he called to her. "And you too, Jether."

"Hi, Mr. Templar!" Jether replied first. "I hoped I'd catch you one last time before you left! Man, I still can't believe how you turned things around in court the other day! It was just incredible!"

"Thank you," Horus nodded cheerfully.

"I mean it!" Jether continued. "Like, the whole time we worked together, you were a total mess! A basket-case, almost! And then, just when you were poised to land flat on your face, you somehow managed to come out looking brilliant! It was the most remarkable thing I ever saw!"

"Thank you," Horus said, not so cheerful this time.

"You have my congratulations as well, Counselor Templar," Dr. Nokkaeru put in. "I have heard at length of your triumphant defeat in court." She shot a look at her nephew. "*Time, and time again*. It is indeed most noteworthy."

"And what of your own affairs, Doctor?" Horus plied, eager to move on and learn something important. "How do things go with the Deputy Constable?"

She looked back at him, then quickly averted. She seemed... quite hesitant... to answer. Horus made ready to repeat his question, when finally, she responded...

"It is a curious story. I find myself... *bewildered*. Much more so even than my impressionable young nephew at your unexpected virtuosity."

"Well now, don't be mysterious," Horus insisted. "Is Milo well? Was he at least able to undergo the procedure?"

"Do not presume to ask those questions as if they are one and the same," she cautioned him. But after her biting remark, she would say nothing more.

"Really, Doctor, you're being impossible," Horus pressed her. "How is he? I must know."

"I would answer your other question first," Nokkaeru replied. "Miloje was found quite unfit for surgery. He could not have survived implantation in his weakened state. His heart was simply too given to its arrythmia. Any sufficiently potent sedative would have certainly caused an arrest in the time it would take to complete the operation. So, he was simply discharged. There was nothing else that could be done for him. *Nothing* at all."

Horus slumped, feeling that Miloje's last hope had come to its worst possible end. Even dying on the operating table would've at least spared him the disgrace of returning home too infirm to function. Now, there was nothing more Blackforest could do to protect him from being found guilty on charges of dereliction of duty. He would be executed by the very state he'd spent his life serving with distinction...

"How dreadful," Horus replied, at length. "I'm... I'm so very sorry for him."

"You may save your sympathy, Templar," an uncanny voice responded. Horus drew himself up out of his defeated posture, searching with an incredulous look. Just then, a man who had been walking nearby removed a travelling hood, revealing himself to be none other than the Deputy Constable... alive, self-propelled... even *vibrant*, if it were possible. But of course, *none* of it should be possible! Even if Nokkaeru had lied outright just now, and the surgery had indeed gone ahead, Miloje would've spent weeks recovering! For him to be here now, on his feet, fairly sauntering...

"You see now why the good Doctor was so loath to discuss my present condition," Miloje continued, even as Horus reeled. "My arrhythmia is quite cured, sans any help from Heron medicine. I have thoroughly frustrated her considerable expertise... and not only hers, but that of her many esteemed colleagues." His mustache didn't hide even a bit of his self-satisfied look.

"It is history's greatest fluke, or I am a fool!" Nokkaeru swore.

Finally, Horus arrived at something that seemed plausible. "But the trade show!" he reminded them. "Remember, there was Life Magic at the trade show! Surely, Milo, you must've sent after some..."

Miloje shook his head, still hopelessly smug. "Wrong as usual, Templar... yet closer to the mark than Nokkaeru here, who would deny me any credit at all for my miraculous recovery." He put a finger to his noggin. "An old inspector still has his guile. Well, I think, she knows it, however she may protest. Suffice it to say, I found a way for myself where she didn't think to look. It may trouble her a good long while yet."

"No, not long," Nokkaeru argued. "Any solution *you* can devise is well within the reach of my wit. It is only a matter of exerting myself to think more artlessly than is my wont. Once I have shed sufficient layers of profundity, I am confident the answer to this despicable riddle of yours will be most apparent."

Miloje gave her a mock bow. "Feel free to prove it, Madam."

"He has been insufferable like this for nearly two days," Nokkaeru returned snapping to Horus. "I felt compelled to monitor him at least until I had him aboard-ship... to be sure he did not suddenly drop dead. But we are nearly to the ramp now, and there seems little hope of that left. So I leave him to *your* care! Why should I bother about it a moment longer? I have other affairs to set in order..."

Horus winced, and not for the first time in this conversation. "You're not coming back with us?"

"Not straight away," Nokkaeru answered. "I had planned on a longer stay than this. But now my patient has unaccountably recovered, and means to return. I say good riddance. Yet I would stay for the duration. It is my privilege." She searched him up and down. "What of you, Counselor? You mean to go now? Your effects suggest you do."

"I *am* leaving now," he replied. "The case is over, and the boat I came on pulls out in a few hours. I see no reason not to be on it."

"Are you *sure*?" she insisted. "What of the council I offered you? What of your meeting with Zedulon? Were you not the least curious what he might have revealed of your future? What he may *still* reveal, if a meeting could be arranged?"

Horus frowned. True to her nature, she couldn't pass up an opportunity to put him on the spot. He *did* still crave some assurances... or, at the least, a clear enough look at the horrors ahead to begin to bulwark himself against them. But he'd turned that offer down once before. Now, he'd just have to do it again...

"I'm sure," he said. "I don't need your Proconsul's prognostication, kindly though you offer it."

"Oh?" Nokkaeru asked, unwilling or unable to simply let the matter lie. "And what, pray tell, would incline you to refuse such coveted insight?"

"A resolution, Doctor, to focus on the present," Horus explained. "If there's anything I've learned over the course of my stay in this country, it's that the present demands our full attention... however we might be tempted to look back, or peer ahead. I'm convinced the past isn't as important as we make it... and any future we spend all our time fretting over is a future worth worrying about. Yesterday's gone, and tomorrow will have to work itself out. There's enough to be done today."

"Rhetorical, as ever, Counselor," Nokkaeru deemed it. "I would say your future remains *quite* worth worrying about, regardless of the ignorance you choose to face it with." She sighed, looking far off ahead of them. "...Although, if you truly had no plans of meeting Zedulon, I suppose it is just as well for you. Another trade show has come and gone without his observance. He never showed."

Horus blinked. "He didn't?"

"No," she answered. "But after all, his coming was only a rumor."

* * *

They continued a short way in silence... just long enough to reach the ship. Why Nokkaeru deigned to make the whole trip after all was beyond Horus' reckoning, unless she really was clinging to the outside chance Miloje would drop dead on the way. Seeing he failed to do so, she turned to go without a word...

"Looks like my aunt's not going to wait-up," Jether said, turning to Horus. "It *was* really cool working for you, Sir... I want you to know that. I hope you don't have so much trouble holding yourself together from here on out. Who knows? You might even go on to pull off another classy loss or two before you get old and die!"

Horus grinned. "Goodbye, boy-wonder," he said. "I'm not sure you learned a single solitary thing from working with me... but I hold out hope for you nonetheless."

Jether nodded. "You took the words right out of my beak, Mr. Templar." Then the boy turned, and in a flurry of wings, he *flew* to catch up with his aunt! Or, well... *maybe* he flew. Almost.

"And so, both baby and babysitter leave us to our own devices at last," Miloje chimed. "Don't feel obliged to fill in for her, Templar. I am really quite my old self, if not improved."

"You're *sure* you don't want a chaperone around anymore, Milo?" Horus joshed him.

Miloje frowned. "You should live long enough to find yourself under so many eyes night and day. Then, perhaps, you'll appreciate my position." He gestured lazily over his shoulder with his thumb. "I'm going aboard now. If I catch you following too close, I may just have to – *discourage* – you."

Horus nodded. "Have it your way, Deputy Constable."

"I usually do, in the end," Miloje called back, already advancing on the ramp. "Yet you people are so often surprised."

Horus just watched him go, forced to applaud the old man's cleverness... though he still had no idea what sort of clever thing he'd done. In any case, the results spoke for themselves. He shook his head, at a loss to imagine... and presently, at a loss for what to do next...

Why the sudden doubt? he wondered. *You were going to board the ship. What's holding you back now?*

Of course, he knew very well what. He was looking for Deborah, even now. He was searching the faces of everyone bunching up around the moors and ramps, hoping against hope he'd find her there. After all, she would've been advised the ship was leaving, as one of its original passengers. And she would've heard the case of *Mobipetrolluck vs. The States* had reached its verdict. He trusted her to be informed of his itinerary, even as he feared to search out any details of her own. His heart sank. Maybe she just couldn't get away. Not even for a brief good-bye. He kicked himself for his arrogance and stupidity... for his cowardice. Why hadn't he gone to say goodbye himself? Why couldn't he just...

Then suddenly, he *found* her... just standing in the amber daylight, looking around nonchalantly with her hands folded, while everyone bustled on their own way. His heart almost punched a hole in one or more hemispheres of his chest. She was *here*!

But just as suddenly, he sank back into despondency, noticing she didn't have her luggage with her...

This really is just a goodbye, he realized...

He sighed a quavering sigh.

Then, he mustered his brave face.

He squared his shoulders and held his ears nice and high.

And he called out...

"Deborah!"

She turned, and smiled. "Horus."

They approached each other.

"I'm glad you're here, Deborah," Horus admitted. "That is... well... I would've understood, if you weren't."

"Wouldn't miss it," she said. Already, her smile began to fade. "I heard how things went. I heard about the guilty verdict. I wanted to let you know, as soon as I could tell you in person... I'm sorry."

Horus chuckled. "Well, you know, there are losses, and there are losses. This one turned out to be quite palatable, in the end. Even Lucky thought so."

She gave him a quizzical look. "Lucky?"

He nodded. "Mo's preferred nickname. He's in for just a short stint in both the Queens' armies. Then it'll be back to his beloved old day job."

At this, the radiance in Deborah's face made a wonderful recovery. "Well in that case, congratulations."

Their brief moment of shared joy evaporated as Horus tried to figure out how to proceed. He reasoned that a prolonged dance around their parting would only maximize the discomfort. So, he skipped right to the chase...

"Speaking of tours of duty... well... I meant to ask if you would write me a brief letter, now and again," he stumbled. *So much for segues*, he thought...

"Oh?" she asked. "I suppose that means I'm going somewhere?"

He frowned, bewildered by the question. "Well, aren't you?"

"In a manner of speaking, yes. I'm getting off this cooky island and going home." Her eyes narrowed. "Where did you *think* I was going?"

Horus hesitated. Finally, he shrugged. "I honestly haven't a clue. To wherever Snozzwell intended to set-up his company's next glorious showcase, I suppose. But in any case, I didn't think you'd be coming back to Jast-Madiir straight away." He nodded at the empty ground around her. "Unless you're travelling much lighter than you came."

She looked around herself, then set her head in her palm. "I already put all my bags on the boat! I didn't think how that would tend to confuse matters."

Horus experienced a wash of relief. She was coming back after all! Even working for Kloggem Mills, at least she might remain headquartered in St. Argonsburg. Surely, he could learn to live with just a visit now and then. It was immeasurably better than what he'd expected...

"I'm so glad to hear it," he admitted. "Perhaps we shan't have to write back and forth after all."

She set a hand on her hip. "There's no 'perhaps' about it, Boss. I'm not paying for postage if I'm going to be working 20 feet from you."

Horus blanched. "You... you mean...?"

"Yes, you big goof!" she laughed at him. "The show's over. I'm going back to work for you, just like Snozzwell said."

I'm going back to work for you. The words echoed in his head, but he could hardly believe he'd actually heard them. Even Miloje's miracle rebound seemed more plausible than this...

"He... did indicate that possibility," Horus agreed at length. "Along with others I thought more likely."

She shrugged. "Maybe I persuaded him to make good on his word. Maybe I threatened him."

He laughed nervously. "*Threatened*?"

"Sure," she replied. "Or maybe all it took was to point out a simple logical paradox. After all, there's no way I can go on being billed as the most famous secretary in the world if I don't secretary anymore."

He stroked his whiskers. "And, he *bought* that? Could it really be so simple?"

"Well, it was either that, or else it was when he discovered the *true* cost of making me the face of Tasty Chunks."

Horus was perplexed. "He had some literal meaning to that?"

"And how. To the tune of having my portrait drawn on *every single* box."

"Expensive?"

"He almost went through the roof."

Horus nodded. "I'm sure it was the cumulative effect of them all." He grabbed up his luggage in one arm, leading her to the ramp with his other hand resting between her shoulders, all the while reflecting. He'd resolved to let her go her own way, however it pained him... and in the end, he got to keep her around anyway. Maybe there was a lesson in there somewhere. Whatever it was, he'd figure it out later...

"Good to have you back, Ms. Boulevard."

"Good to *be* back, Boss."

Together, they boarded the boat, each privately resolving to never again remember the name of Nostradamus Snozzwell...

* * *

Following a thoroughly restful cruise back to St. Argonsburg – where Horus, Deborah, and even Miloje shared plenteous harrowing stories of their personal tribulations on the island of Vathiiki – Horus' return to the real world was both a comfort and, sooner than expected, a reprise of old cares and concerns. In the shadow of so many other fears, Horus had failed to consider some of the potentially dire consequences of losing his case. He remembered only now that Blackforest had conferred on him the Czarina's hope that this trial would help staunch their continual loss of Clerks to the war effort. But of course, he hadn't been able to argue the relevance of Lucky's Jast-Madiir citizenship at all. Setting foot on the dock, he knew right away there was nothing for it. He would go to the SAPD at once, and face the music...

But to his surprise, the DA didn't appear even remotely disappointed at first glance. If anything, he looked deviously pleased...

"Welcome back, Horus... Ms. Boulevard," Blackforest acknowledged them, his razor fangs glistening bright. "Come in, have a seat, take a load off."

Before they could appeal for a brief formal visit, Blackforest took his own invitation, returning to his chair and kicking his feet up on his desk. He unbuttoned his coat as he retrieved his pipe and soap from the inside pockets, mixing up for a good long puff...

"My, but aren't we relaxed today?" Deborah quipped as they also sat down. "What's the occasion?"

"No occasion as such," he explained. "Merely a welcome convergence of every kind of good fortune. The Deputy Constable's back and ready to round-out his tenure. His star pupil and mine just put the final kybosh on the Digit Cults. We've received word of a decisive victory in the war on Despotopia. And, as if the Czarina could be any more pleased, you went and staunched this Clerk shortage up for her brilliantly." He replaced his feet on the ground and stood up, leaning over his desk at Horus with his arm outstretched. "I've been tasked with relaying the personal gratitude of somebody in the Czarina's office myself."

Horus hesitated to accept the handshake, but eventually relented, even as he felt the fur on the back of his neck begin to rise. "Thank you, Hamilton... but I fear there's been some terrible mix up. I lost the case. I didn't establish even the slightest precedent for contesting the conscription of Clerks."

Blackforest nodded. "That's true. But you did something almost as good."

"And what is that?"

"You set the penalty for draft evasion. One death in the military." Blackforest's predatory grin rallied. "In light of this, the Czarina has issued a decree throughout the land: All Clerks are to ignore their draft orders. The foreign authorities are going to have a Heck of a time rounding them up forcibly from here on out. But even if they bother, we should have most of them back in a matter of weeks. Simplicity itself."

Horus smiled. "In that case, you may tell the Czarina's office they're welcome."

Blackforest tipped his pipe. "I'll do just that."

* * *

On their way back through the DA's door, Horus and Deborah happened across Art and Blucille, apparently returning to her office from parts unknown. They watched as Art did a double-take, not seeming to recognize them all at once. Evidently, their return had caught him off-guard...

"Well, Art!" Horus called out. "How nice to see you! Seems that we're always bumping into each other here, when the one you've really come to see is Ms. Cordon."

"Hi, uh, guys," he replied, sounding a bit unsure. "Sorry if I haven't checked-in in a while. I've been, well... busy."

"So have they... out-of-country," Blucille mentioned. "Remember?"

"Oh yeah," he replied.

"We're still getting him caught up on a few things," Blucille explained at Horus and Deborah, giving Art a consoling pat on the arm. Horus wondered at all of this.

"It's been nice," Art added, smiling down at her. "Regular lunch dates with my little Fluffy Face. I'd say we've made up for Friday a few times over by now."

"Made up for it?" Deborah asked. "Don't tell me you had reschedule again?"

Art and Blucille exchanged an uncomfortable look. "We certainly did," Blucille answered, turning to search their faces. "Have the two of you not heard yet?"

"Heard about what?" Horus inquired, growing uneasy.

"Well, things with the undercover job didn't quite go to plan," Art explained on his own behalf. "Those crazy Cultists kinda found out I was a plant. Their secret leader brainwashed me for a week or two."

Deborah and Horus took their turn exchanging a look. "My goodness," Horus breathed. "That's terrible!"

"Yeah, it was bad," Art agreed, pointing at his head. "Left a few holes in the ol' memory bank. But nothing major."

Horus sighed. "And here I thought *we* had a rough go of it. I guess we'll all have plenty to talk about, the next time we can sit and chat."

"How 'bout tonight?" Art suggested. "I have no plans."

Horus nodded. "Alright, its settled. See you then, Art."

"Sure thing." Art patted Horus on the arm. "See ya then, Harry."

Acknowledgments

Ben Stein is owed some thanks here. I'm also going to spotlight my mom again, not just for her customary good work in the proofreading department, but workshopping and character development, too. Thanks go to my dad for suggesting Art's satisfyingly mundane under-cover job. I tended to try to keep Cillian Murphy's Scarecrow in mind as a muse for Bishop Sabracore. Charles Schultz provided me with more ideas than usual on this one as well. Christopher Lee and Jared Harris provided the mental voice-acting of Demicolon and Pseudofluff, respectively. I also rather unabashedly attempted to borrow Lee Arenberg and Mackenzie Crook's POTC characters, though only in writing this postscript, I see I got their names crossed...

Finally, it was a joy to include my rather oblique homage to Carl Held's character in this volume. Thank you, Mr. Gideon. We were never entirely sure what you contributed to the show, and I was only too happy to continue that tradition!

For More from E.L. Ward…

Visit his personal site, at:

https://www.booksofelward.com

His vast arsenal of backlist titles includes the following:

TITLES IN THE ORPHAN UNIVERSE

HERON PROPHECIES SERIES

The Chocolate Prophecy

HORUS TEMPLAR – PUBLIC DEFENDER SERIES

Horus Templar and the Case of the Wimpy War-Criminal
Horus Templar and the Case of the Iniquitous Inquisitor
Horus Templar and the Case of the Draft-Dodging Drone

Made in the USA
Monee, IL
29 January 2022

89856101R00105